Muskegon County

"Partners In Progress" By Earle Berry

PRODUCED IN COOPERATION WITH THE MUSKEGON AREA CHAMBER OF COMMERCE

WINDSOR PUBLICATIONS, INC.
NORTHRIDGE, CALIFORNIA

Muskegon County

Harbor of Promise

An Illustrated History by Jonathan Eyler

To Marcia—without whose help this book, and a lot of other things, could not have been accomplished.

Endsheet: *This is the way the city of Muskegon looked in 1868 during the heyday of its lumbering history. Muskegon Lake was very active, with ships of all descriptions heading to Chicago and Milwaukee markets. Courtesy, Hackley Public Library*

Windsor Publications, Inc.—History Book Division

Publisher: John M. Phillips
Editorial Director: Teri Davis Greenberg
Design Director: Alexander D'Anca

Staff for *Muskegon County: Harbor of Promise*
Senior Editor: Gail Koffman
Editorial Development: Susan L. Wells
Assistant Editors: Laura Cordova, Marilyn Horn
Director, Corporate Biographies: Karen Story
Assistant Director, Corporate Biographies: Phyllis Gray
Editor, Corporate Biographies: Judith Hunter
Sales Representatives, Corporate Biographies: Gordon Obenuf, Calvin Young
Editorial Assistants: Kathy M. Brown, Marcie Goldstein, Pat Pittman, Sharon L. Volz
Designer: Ellen Ifrah
Text Layout Artist: Lori Sandler
Corporate Biographies Layout Artist: Cheryl Carrington

Library of Congress Cataloging-in-Publication Data

Eyler, Jonathan, 1921-
　Muskegon County : harbor of promise.

　"Produced in cooperation with the Muskegon Area Chamber of Commerce."
　Bibliography: p. 196
　Includes index.
　1. Muskegon County (Mich.)—History. 2. Muskegon County (Mich.)—Description and travel. 3. Muskegon County (Mich.)—Industries. I. Muskegon Area Chamber of Commerce (Mich.) II. Title.
F572.M9E94　　1986　　　977.4'57　　　86-9142
ISBN 0-89781-174-7

Contents

Some of the Muskegon "gay blades" are shown on their bicycles in front of Horace Brown's Bicycle Shop at First and Clay in 1892. They were on their way to the Columbian Exposition in Chicago. Courtesy, Charles H. Yates Collection, Muskegon County Museum

Acknowledgments

After some thirty-five years of active newspaper writing, including a smattering of freelancing for magazines, this opportunity to write a book presented itself. It quickly drove me out of a brief retirement of just a little over a year. I am grateful to Windsor Publications, Inc., and especially my editors, Susan L. Wells, and later, Nancy Evans, and Gail Koffman for this challenge.

Being primarily a writer rather than a historian, my approach was to be as general as possible and let the illustrations be more specific. History needn't be dull, as proved by a writer of the caliber of a Bruce Catton, but it sometimes tends to become bogged down with too much attention to dates and details rather than the people who make it.

While not a native of Muskegon, I have lived here long enough and studied enough of the area's history to be impressed with the number of times the city has recovered from major economic blows. It has experienced a roller coaster ride of rags to riches and back to rags again several times in a period of almost 150 years and yet there still are enough people around to continue to try to surmount what seem to be insurmountable problems.

This is not the first history of Muskegon nor do I expect it will be the last. I am grateful to those who have explored the history before me such as Henry H. Holt, Louis H. Conger, John "Lex" Chisholm, Charles H. Yates, J. Fred Boyd and more recently Mrs. Alice Prescott Keys, Frederic Read, and Daniel Yakes and Hugh Hornstein.

I am considerably in debt to a number of people and institutions without whose help this never could have been written. These would include the Hackley Public Library, its director Dale Pretzer and his staff; The Muskegon County Museum, its director Frank Walsh and his staff; Herbert Strum, who knows more about the Hackley House and its restoration than anyone since Charles H. Hackley himself; the *Muskegon Chronicle,* its editor and publisher George Arwady; staffers John Hausman,

The Opera House Orchestra was an integral part of Muskegon's culture for many years. After the Opera House closed, the orchestra continued to entertain at the Lake Michigan Park pavilion. This 1898 photo shows conductor E.J. Aubrey, seated at the left. Courtesy, Charles H. Yates Collection, Muskegon County Museum

David Kolb and others who helped materially or lent a great deal of encouragement; photographer Dave Carlson who spent many hours copying pictures and advising on those that would reproduce and those that would not; and Eleanor Polley of the White Lake Chamber of Commerce. Special thanks are due to librarians Ruth Kirkland, of the Hackley Public Library, and Linda Thompson at the *Muskegon Chronicle* for their diligent and thorough reading of the manuscript for historical accuracy. Then there were many, many friends who constantly expressed interest, asked about the book's progress, and offered encouragement.

I cannot omit my wife, Marcia, who did the typing, some proofreading, was as enthusiastic about the project as I was, and constantly was called upon to revise her schedule to fit mine.

This history may not be the definitive scholarly work, yet it does unravel the highlights of Muskegon's story—in both text and pictures.

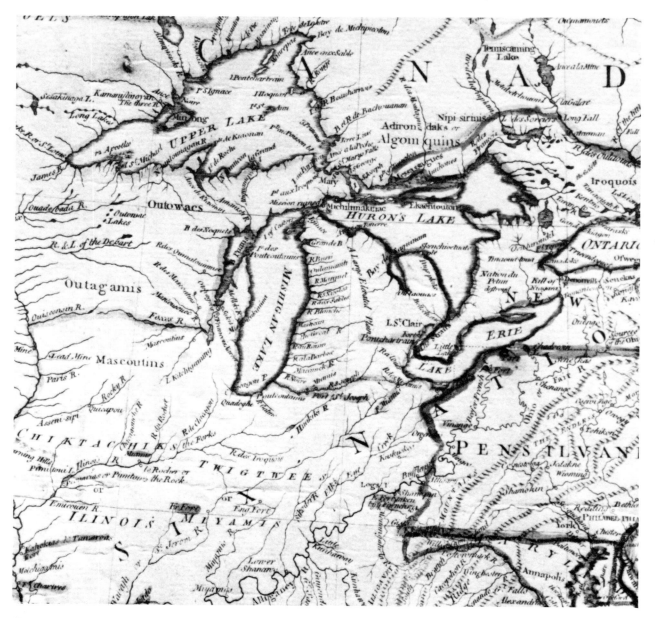

The D'Anville map of 1712 was the first map to show the "Maskigon" River, as the Ottawa Indians called it, or "marshy river." This river, one of the longest waterways in the state, would nurture settlements, the fur trade, and the prosperous lumber industry. Courtesy, Hackley Public Library

1 *In the Beginning*

While the thirteen original colonies were struggling for their independence more than 200 years ago, the rest of the country stretched to the west—a vast panorama of virgin forest, water, and prairies. Michigan was among the areas in this darkened stage waiting for the curtain to rise.

French missionaries and explorers mapped what is now western Michigan in the seventeenth century and from 1622 to 1700 the territory within the borders of Michigan was part of New France. The missionaries came to New France looking for Indian souls to convert while the explorers sought precious metals or anything else of commercial value.

The Muskegon River appeared on early French maps as Masquigon (or Maskigon)—an Ottawa Indian word meaning "marshy river." The Chippewa spelling was Maskego; the present-day spelling wasn't adopted until 1840, after the establishment of Muskegon Township as a part of Ottawa County. The first white men to visit the Muskegon area, long before any settlement there, probably were Pierre Radisson and DesGroseliers, who spent the winter of 1650 on the east shore of Lac des Illinois (the name the early French gave Lake Michigan).

Sault Ste. Marie was the first white settlement in the state. Two Jesuits, Charles Raymbault and Isaac Jogues, visited the site as early as 1641 and Pere Jacques Marquette founded the first permanent settlement there in 1668. Three years later he founded a settlement at St. Ignace.

Robert Cavelier de LaSalle built a fort at the mouth of the St. Joseph River in 1679 and the Sieur de Courtmanche constructed Fort St. Joseph up the river at Niles in 1691. Antoine Cadillac founded the first settlement in the southeastern part of the state at Detroit in 1701. The final French settlement was Fort Michilimackinac, now Mackinaw City, which replaced the abandoned settlement at St. Ignace.

Above: *One of France's great explorers, Robert Cavelier de LaSalle, lost his position in the French court while exploring the Michigan shore on Lake Michigan. He was relieved of his command somewhere off the Muskegon River. Courtesy, Cirker's* Dictionary of American Portraits, Dover, 1967

Left: *Among the first white men to come to Michigan was Jesuit Pere Jacques Marquette. Another of France's great explorers, he probably had his last glimpse of the Great Lakes area near the Muskegon River. He died April 18, 1675, near the outlet of the river now known as the Pere Marquette. Courtesy; Grand Rapids Public Library*

Opposite page: *This is the earliest known map of the Great Lakes region, published in 1703 by the French, during the time when trading was a prosperous occupation. Courtesy, Detroit Public Library*

It is an oddity of history that France's two greatest explorers, Marquette and LaSalle, probably had their last glimpse of the Great Lakes area near the Muskegon River. Legend has it that Marquette saw the dunes at the Muskegon River outlet on April 16 or 17, 1675. He travelled but another fifty miles on his journey home to Michilimackinac when he died April 18, 1675, near the outlet of the river now known as the Pere Marquette. Muskegon's public beach on Lake Michigan is also named after the great Jesuit missionary.

LaSalle's influence in the French court had waned and Chevalier DeBaugis was sent to relieve him. LaSalle, travelling up the Michigan shore on Lake Michigan, learned of his replacement and in 1682 headed for Montreal, enroute to France, but met DeBaugis somewhere off Muskegon and was relieved of his command. He never returned to the Great Lakes.

It is interesting to imagine what passed through the explorers' minds as they gazed upon this wilderness. Their writings do not dwell on the aesthetic beauty they surely observed—the unbroken miles of sandy beaches and impressive dunes, towering pine forests, and unlimited pure water.

These Frenchmen were practical men. They had jobs to do but

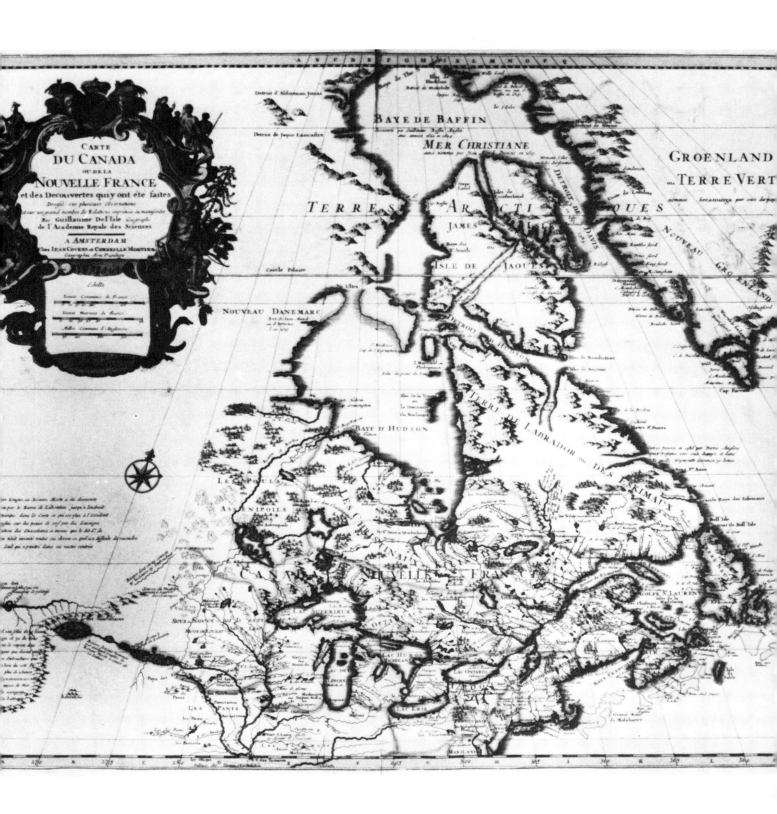

were operating in a region vastly different from their native land. They encountered strange-looking natives and unfamiliar flora and fauna. Perhaps the rigorous tasks of adjusting to and surviving in this remote wilderness kept them from describing the natural beauties they undoubtedly beheld.

They found an area inhabited by three Indian tribes—the Chippewa, Ottawa, and Potowatomi—so closely related in customs, language, and traditions that they were called the "Three Brothers." These tribes were believed to have migrated from Canada in the 1500s and drove the original inhabitants, the Sacs and Foxes, into Wisconsin. The Chippewa were the oldest tribe and lived in the northern part of the Lower Peninsula. The Ottawa were the next oldest and inhabited the valleys of the Muskegon and Grand rivers. The Potowatomi occupied the Kalamazoo River valley and extended around the bottom of Lake Michigan.

In the Indians, the missionaries found fertile ground for their work. Pere Marquette was particularly loved by his Indian "children." The missionaries encountered trouble, however, with fur trade developers. Some of the French traders were unscrupulous in their dealings with the Indians and undermined much of

Right: *The fur trade was the original business of the Muskegon area due to the abundance of wildlife and the numerous waterways to European markets. Pictured here is a French fur trapper of the nineteenth century, one of the few who persevered after trading had virtually ended. Photo by Horace T. Martin, from History and Traditions of the Canadian Beaver*

Opposite page, right: *Chippewa chief, "Rocky Boy," or "Stone Child," is dressed in ornate costume, possibly ceremonial attire. Courtesy, National Archives*

Opposite page, left: *This lithograph is of Chippewa chief "One-Side-of-the-Sky." The Chippewa were one of the three Indian tribes the French explorers encountered in the West Michigan area. The oldest tribe in the region, they lived in the northern part of the Lower Peninsula. Courtesy, State Historical Society of Wisconsin*

the missionaries' accomplishments.

Yet the explorers quickly realized that the fur trade would be their commercial interest in this area. The region abounded in bear, beaver, otter, wolverine, panther, wolf, deer, and vast herds of elk. Numerous waterways provided rapid transportation (for those days) to centers for fur shipments to Europe.

The idea of a few Frenchmen acquiring Indian land never became an issue in those early days. In the brisk fur trade, the white men supplied cloth, cooking and eating utensils, muskets, knives, and other implements needed by the Indians. There was a certain amount of intermarriage and, on the whole, the French and Indians seemed to have lived together in relative peace.

The *coureur de bois* ("runner of the woods"), the French outlaw participating in the fur trade, was very similar to his Indian counterpart. His life was devoted to hunting, fishing, and trapping. He was compatible with the environment but the struggle for food, clothing, and shelter provided only a Spartan existence. There is no evidence that these men were "environmentalists," but most of them soon learned what the Indians knew—to not damage or pollute nature and to take only what was needed for existence.

The entire Indian population of Michigan when the white man came is estimated at 15,000. The number of whites during the fur trade era probably amounted to no more than several hundred.

*　　*　　*

A hundred years before the first white settler came to Muskegon, the area had a great leader in the Ottawa war chief, Pendalouan. "He is a man of great influence in his nation . . . and they do nothing without consulting him," wrote the Marquis De-Boauharnois, Governor General of Canada. The state papers of this period, preserved in Paris archives, record many of the Indian leader's accomplishments.

Pendalouan and his people lived in the "great marsh" (Muskegon) at the mouth of the Muskegon River and Muskegon Lake. The French considered him a staunch ally. He was one of the chiefs who helped the French vanquish the Reynard (Fox) Indians who lived around the foot of Green Bay and controlled the Wisconsin portage to the Mississippi. The Fox tried to form an alliance against the French with the Sioux west of the Mississippi and with the Five Nations in western New York. Had it been successful, this alliance would have entirely severed French lines of communication in the New World.

This elm-bark lodge was the home for the Fox Indians; it was large enough to accommodate several generations of one family. The Fox controlled the Wisconsin portage to the Mississippi until the French drove them out of Wisconsin in 1739. Photo by William S. Prettyman, from Indians: The Great Photographs . . . *by Joanna Cohan Scherer*

The French decided to eradicate the dissident tribe and a strong 1739 expedition, reinforced by war parties of Indian allies, drove the Fox out of Wisconsin and brought them to bay at Starved Rock on the Illinois River. After a month-long seige, the Fox tried to escape in June 1739, but were virtually wiped out. The jubilant French returned to Montreal, where they bestowed presents on their Indian allies and conferred high honors on the war chiefs. Among the most signally honored was Pendalouan.

A man of strong character and independent mind, Pendalouan had second thoughts about the appalling fate of the Fox tribe. He succeeded in having the few survivors adopted into other tribes rather than massacred. The prolonged defiance of the French by the Foxes had its effect on leaders of other subservient tribes, and the French became greatly alarmed.

Pendalouan was officially rebuked for his sympathy to the Fox, and he, in reply, scornfully threw his French medals of honor into the river. He was deposed as chief, but his influence among the Indians continued and the French soon found it necessary to restore him to favor. Pierre Joseph Sieur DeBlainville, in command at Ft. Michilimackinac, was designated to bring him back into the fold. The French wanted the Ottawa to move close to Mackinac where they could be kept from the influence of the *coureurs du bois* and English. But fur animals along the Muskegon River had been hunted out so the Indians wanted to move

French fur traders supplied the Indians with cloth, cooking and eating utensils, muskets, knives, and other supplies. Picture by Coke Smith. Courtesy, Royal Ontario Museum

to the Grand River or Grand Traverse.

In a speech to the chiefs, DeBoauharnois told the Indians at Muskegon:

That land is in no wise [sic] suited to you because of the frequent maladies [malaria was the most common] which prevail at that place which may destroy you. Moreover, it ruins your hunting, and you must have observed that when you spend the summer at that place, you scatter the animals and thus render the hunting less productive. The point in question, my children, is for you to settle in a place where you may find good land capable of yielding profitable crops, in order to enable you to secure subsistence for your families and reclaim your hunting grounds.

DeBoauharnois recommended they settle at L'Arbre Croche (above Harbor Springs). The Indians still refused to move, preferring Grand Traverse if they had to be relocated. DeBlainville redoubled his efforts to bring Pendalouan back into the fold and succeeded to the extent that the chief made every effort to induce his nation to adopt the L'Arbre Croche location. In 1742, just two years later, they did.

The following summer, Pendalouan went to Montreal and was restored as chief. He and his tribe never returned to Muskegon from the Little Traverse region, in the northern section of the Lower Peninsula.

*   *   *

During the war between the French and English in America, the settlements in Michigan passed to English control—Detroit in 1760 and the others in 1761. The white inhabitants, mostly French, sought homes elsewhere because they were subjected to English rule until the Quebec Act of 1774.

The British made an administrative mistake in abolishing the French fur trading monopolies, giving independent traders full reign. This opened the way for an excess of cheating, fraud, and dishonesty that infuriated the Indians. The Indians, who had been allies of the French, were so badly treated by both English officers and traders that Pontiac, chief of the Ottawa, attacked Fort Detroit. The fort was besieged for 115 days. Aroused by Pontiac's example, other Indians took Fort St. Joseph and Fort Michilimackinac.

The capture of Fort Michilimackinac is a well-recounted story of a modern "Trojan horse." The Indians proposed a lacrosse game outside the fort to entertain the English garrison. The

Opposite page: *This painting is of Chief Pontiac of the Ottawa tribe. Pontiac attacked Fort Detroit in protest of the ill treatment of the Indians by the English. This seige prompted other Indians to take forts St. Joseph and Michilimackinac. Courtesy, Detroit Historical Museum*

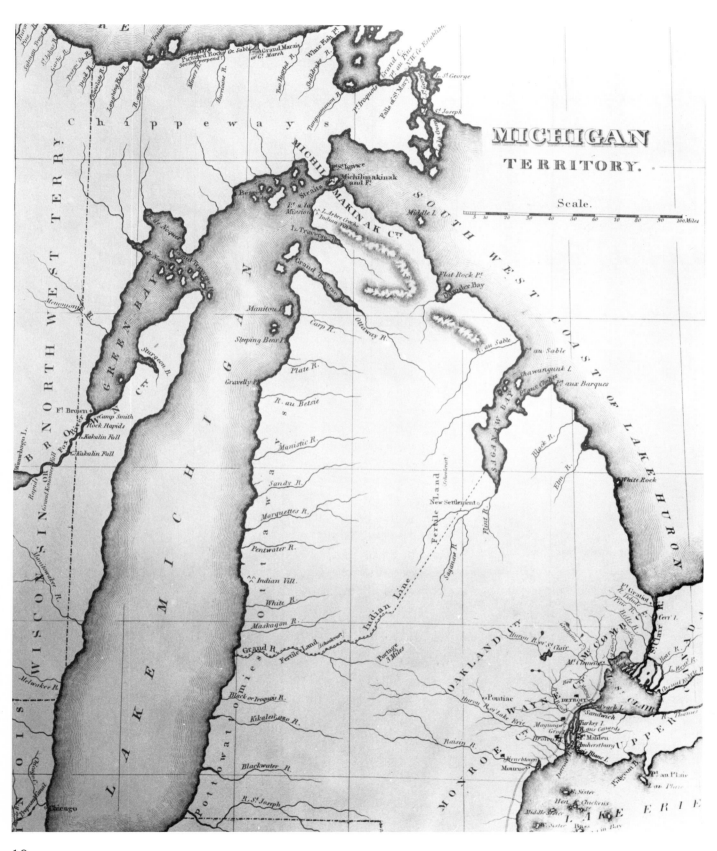

squaws clustered near the gate with concealed weapons in their clothing while hundreds of yelling braves amused the British with the game. An Indian then "accidentally" threw the ball over the stockade and the mob of players went in pursuit. They picked up their weapons from the squaws and quickly subdued the garrison after storming the gate.

At the close of the American Revolution, title of what is now Michigan passed to the United States. In 1778 the region became part of the Northwest Territory; in 1803 the area became part of the Indiana Territory. Two years later it was organized into the Michigan Territory, consisting of the Lower Peninsula and an east-end strip of the Upper Peninsula.

Michigan again passed under British rule during the War of 1812. Commodore Oliver Hazard Perry's victory on Lake Erie (September 10, 1813) won it back for the United States, except for the Mackinac area which was not regained until 1815. Not until November 11, 1828, did the British garrison quit Drummond Island—the last English troops to leave the United States.

Up until 1815 the territory remained mostly wilderness with fur trading the main occupation. The few small settlements were confined to the borders. Inaccurate reports by surveyors sent to the United States government described the interior of Michigan as a vast swamp with only small, scattered pieces of land fit for cultivation. Michigan's white population was only 3,106 in 1800 but increased rapidly with the influx of settlers.

Settlers differed from trappers in that they were interested in settling permanently. This involved clearing the land for farming and establishing home industries like blacksmithing and milling. They also established towns.

The opening of the Erie Canal in 1815 made the Michigan land accessible to settlers. The price of land was then only $1.25 an acre. About this time three roads were built which traversed the Lower Peninsula from east to west. One of these, authorized by Congress in 1832, was known as the "Grand River Road." It ran from Detroit through Pontiac into Shiawassee County and then west to Newton (now Grand Haven) at the mouth of the Grand River. A railroad was later constructed along the same route. Many of the early settlers came from New England looking for new land to farm after battling with the stubborn, stony soils of the Northeast. There was also an influx of immigrants from Europe—mostly English, Irish, and Scandinavians.

The population of Michigan jumped to 31,640 in 1830, 87,278 in 1834, and 174,543 at the time of the first state census of 1860. This census showed 6,172 American Indians while 3,657 were classified as "civilized Indians," meaning they had some

Opposite page: This early map of the Michigan Territory, dated 1822, shows the three local rivers—the Pentwater, White, and Muskegon. This map was drawn before Muskegon even existed as a village. Courtesy, Hackley Public Library

contact with settlers and lived near settlements.

The Indians made many vital contributions to the early white settler in this area. They were his guides in early days; provided furs as the chief article of commerce for almost 200 years; taught him to raise corn, the principal food of the pioneer; introduced him to tobacco (now a controversial benefit); taught him canoe construction—the chief means of rapid transportation in those days and they made the trails which eventually became the main highways of civilization.

In the early 1800s the government became interested in acquiring Indian lands and the methods used became one of the sorriest chapters in the history of this country. There was little advance planning and even less thought about the future of these land purchases. The government recognized only that the Indians "owned" the land and set about to acquire great chunks of it in any way possible. This gave the Indian the option of adopting his century-old culture to the white man's, or moving on. In a little over fifty years there was no place left to "move on" to and the Indian was thus stuck with a way of life he neither understood nor wanted.

In 1821 the lands south of the Grand River were ceded to the United States by the Indians. The government agreed to pay the Ottawa $1,000 annually forever and to appropriate $1,500 each year for ten years to support a blacksmith, teacher, and agriculture instructor and to purchase cattle and farming implements for the reservation.

The lands north of the Grand River were ceded March 28, 1836, after a long conference in Washington between the government and Indian chiefs. The Indians were to receive an annuity of $30,000 for twenty years, $18,000 of it to be paid to Indians between the Grand River and Cheboygan; $5,000 a year for education, $3,000 for mission, $10,000 for agricultural implements, cattle, and mechanical tools, and $300 for medicines and a physician.

Every year for twenty years the Indians north of the Grand River were to be given provisions to the amount of $2,000 plus 6,500 barrels of tobacco, 100 bushels of salt, and 500 barrels of fish. A sum of $300,000 was set aside to pay the debts of Indians and $150,000 as a fund for half-breeds. They also were given two additional blacksmith shops, a permanent interpreter, two farmers, and two mechanics to instruct them. They were promised $150,000 in goods on ratification of the treaty and $200,000 extra if they chose to give up their reservations. The government also agreed to move the Indians west if they desired and to pay for mission establishment on the Grand River.

Above: *White Bear was a Potowatomi chief among the principal chiefs who visited Washington, D.C., in 1857 as representatives of their tribes. He most likely received this suit during the delegation trip. Courtesy, Smithsonian Institution*

Opposite page: *Indian agent Henry R. Schoolcraft signed the Grand River treaty for the United States on March 28, 1836, after a long conference between the government and Indian chiefs. This treaty ceded lands north of the Grand River to the government. Courtesy, Michigan State Archives, Department of State*

The Old Indian Cemetery on Morris Street was given to Muskegon City by Martin Ryerson's son, Martin A. Ryerson. It was thought at one time that the senior Ryerson's first wife, an Indian, was buried here, but test drillings have failed to show any human remains. Photo by David Carlson. Courtesy, David Carlson

The treaty was signed by Henry Schoolcraft for the United States government and for the Indians by Muskegon area chiefs.

Tribal organization finally was dissolved about 1855 and seventeen bands of Ottawa numbering between 1,300 and 1,400 were moved from the Muskegon-Grand Haven area to grants in Elbridge Township in Oceana County.

Chief Cob-Moo-Sa, who ranks with Pendalouan as one of the foremost Indian leaders in the Muskegon area, stated the case for the Indians prior to his death in 1872:

I am an Indian and can be nothing else. I wish my people and my children to be civilized. I know that your ways are superior to mine and that our people must adopt them or die. But I cannot change. The old cannot adopt new ways. You can bend the young tree, but not the old oak.

*   *   *

Muskegon's "white" history apparently began about 1812. During the war with England two traders were captured on the shore of Lake Michigan and taken to Detroit as prisoners of war. They were Joseph Bailey, owner of a trading post near the mouth of the Grand River, and E. Lamarandie, whose post was near the Muskegon Lake outlet. Also in 1812, John Baptiste Recollet had a trading post approximately twenty rods, or about 110 yards, west of the mouth of Bear Lake. Another trading post, established by a Mr. Constant at Bluffton, was occupied for about thirty years.

Bailey's trading post was maintained until 1834 when he sold it to Louis Baddeau, who is credited with being the first permanent resident in Muskegon. Very few trappers maintained any kind of residence the year round. They usually arrived in autumn, stayed the winter buying furs, then left for the trading centers in the spring.

The second permanent settler in Muskegon was Joseph Troutier (known as "Truckee"), who erected a building of hewn lumber on the banks of Muskegon Lake in 1835 and occupied it for several years. Troutier was among those who went to Washington to assist in the writing of the 1836 treaty with the Indians.

Some early white settlers were buried in the Old Indian Cemetery; their remains were later moved to other cemeteries. Estimates of the number of Indians buried in the cemetery range up to sixty but a 1960 excavation failed to turn up any remains. Nevertheless, it remains today as Muskegon's oldest monument to its oldest inhabitants.

WHITE LAKE AREA INDIAN LEGENDS

While Pendalouan ranks as the most famous Indian in the Muskegon area's history, the White Lake area produced several other interesting chiefs and legends.

It is estimated that there were between 4,000 to 6,000 Indians in the area when the white man came to White Lake. The Indians had cleared about 800 acres of land to raise their corn, squash, and pumpkin. They raised wild rice and various berries in the marshes. There were plenty of animals and fish available for food.

The Potowatomies seem to have been the original settlers of the area. Nearly two centuries ago, an aged Potowatomie woman, then believed to have been nearly 100 years old, told the saga of her people and a village which was destroyed in a battle about 1642.

The Potowatomies had their village located on the northern end of what is now the Cockerill Farm in White River Township, covering more than twenty acres. The Potowatomie woman said this was the site of a large village where her people lived and were attacked by "the enemy" which, after cutting off their water supply, forced the inhabitants to flee down the Indian trail to Indian Point where the final massacre occurred.

French Jesuit writings of 1644 give this account: The long struggle between the so-called "Neutral Nation" and the "Nation du Feu" (Potowatomies) was continuing with unabated fury. Father Jerome Lalemant, a Jesuit of the time, reported that in the summer of 1642 the Neutrals, with a force of some 2,000 warriors, advanced into the country of the Nation du Feu and attacked a village of this tribe which was strongly defend-

Shabbona, or "Built Like a Bear," was another principal Potowatomi chief. He was also the grandnephew of the Ottawa tribe's Chief Pontiac. Courtesy, Smithsonian Institution

ed by palisades and manned by some 900 to 1,000 warriors. The Potowatomi defenders withstood the attack for about ten days but then the water supply was shut off and the place overrun. Many of the defendants were killed on the spot while some were taken captive; others escaped only to be captured, tortured, and burned at the stake.

(The Neutral Indians were a tribe that did not join the Six Nations in their fight against the English. They were called Neutral because they were friendly to whites and seldom made war against them. The Neutrals and Ottawas were of Iroquois stock and drove the Potowatomies into Wisconsin but the conquerors fell before disease, fighting, and the white man's whiskey. The Potowatomies returned, but only to be driven away again by the Ottawas in 1825, this time to the south of St. Joseph and into Illinois.)

Many prominent Indians were buried and mounds were raised to mark the spots. The largest mound was built on a high hill above Silver Creek and believed to be the burial place of Chief Owasippe. According to legend, Owasippe had two teenage sons in whom he took great pride. They liked to hunt and fish and sometimes went far down the river in search of game. On one of these expeditions they failed to return after a

reasonable length of time and the chief became anxious over their whereabouts. Every day he climbed the high hill and sat for hours beneath a great pine tree scanning the long marsh and watched for the reappearance of his beloved sons. But the two boys were never again seen and eventually the father succumbed. His people found him dead beneath the great pine and so built his mound where he had kept such a long vigil.

In the early 1890s three boys were following the trail at the mouth of Silver Creek when they noticed something like the end of a canoe protruding from the bank. They hurried back to town and notified the village marshal who went back with some men armed with shovels. They unearthed two dugouts, each containing the skeleton of a teenaged Indian, and there were metal parts of a flintlock gun, bits of decayed blankets, a copper kettle, and a silver ornament. The place is now named Burying Ground Point, since the boys thought they had found an Indian burial ground, but it has since been believed that this was the fate of Owasippe's sons. They apparently had pulled their canoes up to the bank for the night and the river, constantly cutting into the earth, had caused it to cave in, burying them while they slept.

These men are floating logs down the Muskegon River during a river drive. This was an arduous and hazardous job—the slightest error in positioning the logs could bring on a major logjam that would take several hours, and sometimes dynamiting, to break up. Courtesy, Lightfoot Collection, Michigan Collections, Bentley Historical Library, University of Michigan

2 *Daylight in the Swamp*

The fur trade, which the Indians, French, and English thought would never end, came to a close in the Muskegon area in the 1830s. Next in line for exploitation were the vast forests of white pine, also thought to be inexhaustible.

Even though Muskegon village was not incorporated until 1861, the founding of Muskegon is dated 1837—the same year Benjamin H. Wheelock constructed the first sawmill in the area. Although Muskegon's lumber industry lasted only slightly longer than fifty years, it was historically Muskegon's most important era, establishing the city as the most significant on Lake Michigan's east shore and the equal to Chicago as a port.

There were several factors which made lumber Muskegon's big business. First was the type of trees available. North of a line running roughly from Muskegon to Saginaw, the character of timber changed from predominantly hardwoods to softwoods. Chief among these was the white pine with large stands of cork, long or pumpkin pine. These trees grow from 125 to 175 feet in height and two-and-a-half to five feet in diameter. Some grow as tall as 200 feet and measure seven feet in diameter. The wood is light which makes it float easily, is free of knots and imperfections, and produces beautiful cream-colored wood.

Secondly, the climate was ideal for logging. Cold winters froze the swampy areas and provided snow on which to build logging roads from the cuts to the rivers. Spring thaws provided ample water for the log drive to the mills.

Thirdly, the Muskegon River is one of the longest in Michigan, originating in Higgins Lake in the north-central part of the state. From there it flows into Houghton Lake and winds for some 300 miles until it reaches Muskegon Lake. The river and its tributaries drain an area of several thousand square miles.

Another factor, which did not manifest itself until a later date, was the ease of lumber transport by ship to Chicago and subse-

This circa 1900 photograph illustrates how Muskegon's cold winters helped the logging industry. Logging roads were built from the cuts to the rivers; once the ice melted, the logs were driven downriver. Courtesy, Lightfoot Collection, Michigan Collections, Bentley Historical Library, University of Michigan

quent shipment by rail to the rapidly developing middlewestern farms and towns.

The time was also ripe. Ruthless logging in Maine and in eastern Michigan had denuded large areas of forests and the relentless loggers moved west in search of other fertile territory.

Wheelock was the agent of the Muskegon Steam Company, most of the stockholders of which resided in Detroit and Ann Arbor. The sawmill was begun in January 1837 on a site nearly opposite the old Muskegon Cracker Company (now opposite Shaw-Walker on Muskegon Lake). The Panic of '37 interrupted the mill's construction; it was finally completed and its first lumber sawed in 1838. A fairly large mill for the time, it used two upright or sash saws. The mill was equipped with the boilers and engine of the steamboat *Chicago* which was wrecked near St. Joseph in 1836.

However, the sawmill did not prove to be a profitable venture and it passed into the hands of John Lloyd of Grand Rapids and John P. Place of Ionia. The two owned and operated it until it burned in 1841. The machinery was taken to Grand Rapids.

In August 1837 Jonathan H. Ford, the agent of the Buffalo and Black Rock Company, began building a water mill at the mouth of Bear Lake. Completed the next year, its first cargo of lumber was hauled to the mouth of Muskegon Lake and put on

Opposite page, top: *This enormous load of logs weighed in at 10,000 feet on the log scale. Despite the size of the load, a team of horses could easily move it over an iced logging road. The photograph was taken in 1887. Courtesy, William J. Brinen Collection*

Opposite page, bottom: *Teams of oxen were the first method used to haul logs out of the woods. They were later replaced by horses and then railroads. Courtesy, The Muskegon Collection, Hackley Public Library*

Below: *The schooner* Lyman M. Davis *was a fixture for many years in Muskegon harbor. It was used primarily to carry lumber to Chicago markets. Courtesy, Muskegon Chronicle*

board the schooner *Victor* for Chicago. Some 40,000 feet were loaded and the ship finally reached Chicago after a long, cold, and disagreeable voyage. The vessel was held for some time in the grip of an ice floe and it took ten days to reach its destination. The crew suffered from cold and hunger but had the distinction of delivering the first cargo of lumber from Muskegon to Chicago.

Hiram Judson and Company purchased the mill in 1840 and made extensive repairs and improvements. These included installing a new waterwheel made by George Ruddiman. The mill was valued at $20,000 and was the best on the lake for several years. It burned in 1853 and was never replaced.

Theodore Newell began to build a mill in the spring of 1838 and finished it in 1839. It had but one upright saw and could cut only 6,000 feet of lumber in twenty-four hours. The engine was relatively small and did not have the power to haul up a log while cutting one at the same time. In September 1845 Martin Ryerson and J.H. Knickerbocker bought the mill and removed it the following winter, built a new one on the site, and had it running within three months. In 1847 Knickerbocker sold his inter-

est to Robert W. Morris who continued in partnership with Ryerson until 1865 when the firm became Ryerson, Hills and Company.

By 1850 there were six sawmills on Muskegon Lake with an aggregate capacity of 60,000 feet of lumber per day. Ten more mills were added in the next ten years.

Despite its importance in the lumber business, Muskegon remained an out-of-the-way place; to reach it in those early days one had to arrive by boat or along the shore. Henry H. Holt, in his 1876 *Centennial History of Muskegon,* describes how Alfred A. Maxim came to Muskegon in November 1843. Maxim came from Kenosha, Wisconsin, by schooner to Grand Haven with two yoke of oxen and some men he had employed to seek his fortune in lumbering:

After reaching Grand Haven he started along the beach of Lake Michigan for Muskegon, there being at the time no road through

Opposite page: *Henry H. Holt, Muskegon's first historian, went as far as any local person in politics. He served two terms as lieutenant governor of Michigan in 1872 and 1874. He also served three terms in the state legislature in 1866, 1870, and 1886. Courtesy, The Muskegon Collection, Hackley Public Library*

Below: *Ryerson, Hills and Company, another of Muskegon's large lumber firms, operated the Bay Mill, now the site of the Muskegon State Park picnic and boat launch area. This photo shows the company boardinghouse, store, and office at Bay Mill. Courtesy, William J. Brinen Collection*

This early map, circa 1880, of Muskegon and the surrounding area shows how the outlying property was divided in acreage with the names of the owners. Since the early nineteenth century there have been several attempts at political consolidation of the Muskegon area, but all were unsuccessful. Greater Muskegon now includes Muskegon, Muskegon Heights, North Muskegon, Norton Shores, and Roosevelt Park as well as Muskegon and Laketon townships. Courtesy, Jonathan Eyler

the woods. They had not proceeded far when they came to a place where the driftwood had filled up the narrow space between the water and a high bank; and not being able to drive around, they were obliged to unload the wagons—part of the load being barrels of pork—take apart the wagons, and carry them and the contents over the hill. They then led the oxen around, and having yoked them and put the wagons together, loaded up and started again.

Mr. Maxim was entirely unacquainted with quicksand, and when driving along the smooth sand at the mouth of Little Black Lake, the oxen began to sink, and before he could get up on dry land they had sunk so far that their heads alone were visible. After great exertion they finally succeeded in rescuing the animals alive from their perilous situation. They left the beach at the mouth of Black Lake and went through the woods, taking their course by compass, and reached Muskegon Lake near where the A.V. Mann and Co. mill is located. From there they followed up the lake and stopped at the Muskegon House, then kept by Mr. Dill. These wagons were the first ever driven into Muskegon.

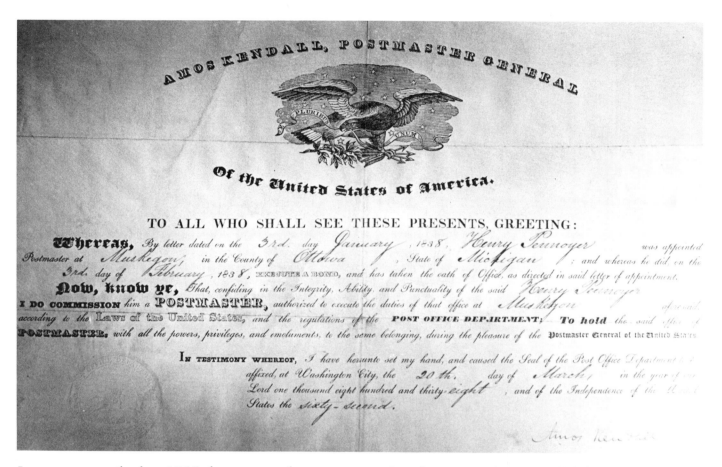

AMOS KENDALL, POSTMASTER GENERAL

Of the United States of America.

TO ALL WHO SHALL SEE THESE PRESENTS, GREETING:

Whereas, By letter dated on the 3rd. day January, 1838, Henry Pennoyer was appointed Postmaster at Muskegon, in the County of Ottawa, State of Michigan: and whereas he did, on the 3rd day of February, 1838, execute a bond, and has taken the oath of Office, as directed in said letter of appointment.

Now, know ye, That, confiding in the Integrity, Ability, and Punctuality of the said Henry Pennoyer I do commission him a POSTMASTER, authorized to execute the duties of that office at Muskegon aforesaid, according to the Laws of the United States, and the regulations of the POST OFFICE DEPARTMENT; To hold the said office of POSTMASTER, with all the powers, privileges, and emoluments, to the same belonging, during the pleasure of the Postmaster General of the United States.

In testimony whereof, I have hereunto set my hand, and caused the Seal of the Post Office Department to be affixed, at Washington City, the 20th. day of March, in the year of our Lord one thousand eight hundred and thirty-eight, and of the Independence of the United States the sixty-second.

Amos Kendall

It was not until after 1855 that a stage line was started and a road was cut through the woods and swamps to Ferrysburg.

*   *   *

In December 1837, at the onset of the lumber boom, Muskegon became a township. The legislature of the newly-formed state of Michigan set aside the territory embracing the present townships of Muskegon, Laketon, Norton, Fruitport, Moorland, Egelston, Ravenna, Chester, and Casnovia and named it the Township of "Maskegon." At the next session of the legislature in 1838, the act was amended to change the spelling to "Muskegon."

The first town meeting was held in 1838 with Henry Penoyer elected supervisor. The first land entry was by a Mr. Taylor who built a shanty on Lot 1, section 19, in December 1836. He sold the property to Horace Wilcox, who perfected the entry of the land. He, in turn, sold it to Theodore Newell, who platted it in 1849. The property lay roughly on either side of Pine Street between Muskegon Lake and Webster Avenue. Nothing was done with this plat for several years, most likely due to the hill at the

This paper established the first Muskegon post office January 3, 1838, with Henry Pennoyer as postmaster. Pennoyer was also the first supervisor of Muskegon Township while it was still part of Ottawa County. Courtesy, Hackley Public Library

Postmen first began carrying mail in Muskegon July 1, 1860. The six carriers and their superintendent, W.J. Waller (center rear with derby hat), are here pictured. Courtesy, Charles H. Yates Collection, Muskegon County Museum

corner of Pine and Western which was so steep a man could not ascend, even on horseback.

An early sign of civilization was the establishment of a post office on January 3, 1838, at the mouth of Muskegon Lake—at that time the central location for settlers along the lake. The mail was brought up from Grand Haven occasionally by Indians. A three-day-a-week service was established in the late 1840s but daily mail service did not start until 1860. The post office eventually was moved to the "head of the lake," as the present site of Muskegon was then designated. But business was so insignificant that it was discontinued February 11, 1847. It was reestablished March 2, 1848, with George W. Walton appointed postmaster.

Soon following the post office came schools and churches. The first school in Muskegon was a private one taught by a Miss Clark in the winter of 1848-49, in a room in the home of Charles Martin.

Above: *Mrs. Salem Swayze was familiar to all Muskegon schoolchildren in the late 1800s. She taught penmanship, a subject which has long since gone out of fashion. Courtesy, Charles H. Yates Collection, Muskegon County Museum*

Left: *An educator who was familiar to most Muskegon public schoolchildren was Miss Addie M. Bates, principal of Central School before it burned in 1890. She later married S.C. Moon and was principal of Hackley School for a time, where there is a stone monument erected in her memory. Courtesy, Charles H. Yates Collection, Muskegon County Museum*

The first schoolhouse erected was built by private subscription in the autumn of 1849, on the corner of Clay and Terrace. It was twenty by thirty feet, one story high, and cost about $300. It was later considerably enlarged and was for several years the village's only schoolhouse and place for religious services. It was finally sold, removed, and converted into Holt's Hall which was destroyed in the great fire of August 1, 1874.

The first Union School building was erected in 1860. After much debate, a site was selected where the current Muskegon School Administration building is located. Then followed a long controversy over heating. The architect suggested the building be heated by a central furnace. Local stove dealers violently opposed this, arguing that furnaces were unreliable and fire hazards. Indignant citizens took up the cry and the building ultimately was heated by seven stoves—Muskegon was not going to take any chances with such an apparatus as a furnace!

Muskegon citizens also argued over the location of the school

Right: *This is the church VanPammel built at First Street and Clay Avenue, St. Mary's Catholic Church. Father VanPammel baptized an infant in the church in 1856, the same year it was constructed. Courtesy, The Muskegon Collection, Hackley Public Library*

Opposite page: *Father Frederick Baraga, a Roman Catholic priest, built the first church in Muskegon in 1832, out of tree trunks and branches on a hill overlooking Lake Michigan and the Muskegon Lake outlet. He blessed the place on April 20, 1834, then preached to a group of Indians and white men. Courtesy, Grand Rapids Public Library*

building on the square. It finally was decided that the building should be located at the intersection of lines drawn across the block. The frame building Union School was completed in 1862, equipped with seven stoves, each surrounded by a tin-sheet barricade.

The church first made its appearance in 1832 when Frederick Baraga, a Roman Catholic priest, built a crude structure of tree trunks and branches on a hill overlooking Lake Michigan and the Muskegon Lake outlet at Port Sherman. He blessed the place on April 20, 1834, and preached to a group of Indians and a few white men. Father Baraga was at that time the first priest in Grand Rapids and was succeeded in 1835 by Father Vizorky, a Hungarian missionary priest.

Father Vizorky held a Roman Catholic service with Mass in the trading post of William Lasley in the fall of 1835 at the corner of Eighth and Western where the Hackley and Sons office and Hackley and Hume mills were later located. After his death in Grand Rapids in 1853, he was succeeded by Father Edward VanPammel, who came from Belgium where he had been ordained the year previously. There was no road to Muskegon at the time of VanPammel's first visit in 1853, and all travelers had to

Opposite page: *The Methodist Episcopal Church was one of the first Protestant churches in Muskegon. The wooden sidewalks and sawdust streets indicate that this photo was taken before 1870. Courtesy, The Muskegon Collection, Hackley Public Library*

Right: *When lumber camps advanced from crews of eight men to up to 100, the number of buildings increased to include stables, a blacksmith shop, bunkhouse for the men, cook house, and dining room. Courtesy, Charles H. Yates Collection, Muskegon County Museum*

journey through Grand Haven and along the beach. VanPammel visited Muskegon several times a year and in 1855 began his efforts to build a church where the increasing number of Catholics could worship.

VanPammel purchased land at what is now the corner of First and Clay. The tract was covered by thick forest; trees had to be felled to provide space for the small church building, thirty feet long and twenty feet wide. The lumber was rough and had been cut in the waterpower sawmill of George Ruddiman at the mouth of Ruddiman Creek. Constructed in 1856, the church's interior was rustic and unfinished. Planks were laid across blocks of wood to provide seats. Father VanPammel baptized an infant in the new church September 8, 1856. The first complete service was held in 1857 and the first rectory for priests built in 1859.

The first Protestant service in Muskegon was held on the fourth Sunday in October 1840 by Reverend J. Wilcox, a minister of the Congregational Church in Genessee, Illinois. The service was held in the Newell and Wilcox mill boardinghouse at Eastern and Western where the oldest part of the now-defunct Norge Hotel stood. In 1843 a Methodist minister conducted a service in Muskegon at the same boardinghouse, although it was by then enlarged and the mill was managed by Martin Ryerson.

Until 1850 religious services were held at intervals whenever some minister happened to come to the settlement.

In the summer of 1850 a Congregational minister at Lamont —near Grand Rapids—agreed to come to Muskegon on alternate Sundays and did so through the summer and part of the following winter. Services were held in the new schoolhouse on the northwest corner of Clay and Terrace. The Congregational Society of Muskegon was organized April 7, 1859, and the First Congregational Church was formed in June of that same year.

*   *   *

As the settlement grew, lumbering continued to be the main occupation. When all the timber near the lake and mills had been cut, companies bought large tracts of timber up the Muskegon River, beginning around 1847-48. This divided the industry into three distinct jobs: the logger or lumberjack, who cut the timber in the woods; the driver or river hog, who got the logs down the river to Muskegon Lake (and was usually a logger in the winter); and the millhand, who sawed the logs into lumber in the Muskegon mills. Lumbering provided many other jobs

A group of rivermen pose aboard a raft carrying their cook shanty, circa 1880. The cook was considered the most important man because he kept the crew fed. He was also considered the boss as he settled disputes and kept order among the men. Courtesy, Grand Rapids Public Library

Although this picture is undated and the site unknown, these were typical lumberjacks or loggers, who cut the timber in the woods of Muskegon. Little changed in the dress of lumberjacks over the years, from the 1840s to the 1880s. Courtesy, Muskegon Chronicle

within the growing community.

Logging operations started as small, individual enterprises. In those days when land cost only $1.20 an acre—including timberland—a lumberman often purchased forty or eighty acres. He usually picked a plot with a meadow where he could grow hay in the summer to feed his livestock in the winter. The lumberman had four yoke of oxen plus one "spare" ox; that way, if anything happened to one of his animals he could replace it without going to town.

The other part of the lumberman's team was an eight-man crew. This eight-man crew consisted of a foreman, two swampers, three loaders, a teamster, and a cook. The foreman nearly always was the chopper. His duty was to fell the tree and trim off its lower limbs. The swampers used a crosscut saw to saw the tree into proper lengths. They also cleared brush from the road so the teams could have easy access to the riverbank. The loaders piled the logs on sleds, usually about twelve feet wide. A sled load usually consisted of six to eight logs. The teamster drove the logs to the riverbank where they would be kept for the spring drive. The final crew member was the cook—an important man because he kept the crew fed. He also was considered the boss of the crew in that he settled disputes and kept order among the men.

About 75 percent of the men were from Maine. They were the best loggers around and were called "blue noses." Other loggers were from Nova Scotia, New Brunswick, and occasionally France. But the "blue noses" were the best in the business.

Like the crews, the camps did not vary from one to the next. The buildings were all twenty by forty feet. At one end was a door and at the other end a window. The sides were about four feet high made of logs and there was a sloping roof made of split logs, covered with brush and a top filling of dirt.

To one side of the door was the "dingle" where the tools were stored. On the other side was the storehouse, filled with provisions and kept locked by the cook. Under an opening in the center of the roof was the fireplace. On either side of the fireplace was a bunk in which four men slept, all with their feet to the fire. In front of the fireplace was a bunk seat known as the "deacon's seat" where the men dried their shoes at night, told stories, and smoked.

In the rear of the building was the dining table. The men ate well, though simply. Flour, corn meal, sugar, and beans formed the greater part of the camp provisions. They also used great quantities of dried apples and salt pork. Bread was baked in a reflector oven facing the fireplace.

In October the lumberman would take his crew and a wagon loaded with temporary supplies into his cutting area. The men would not see civilization again until the next spring. In spring then, the crews in several camps along the river would join forces

The bateaux crew was an important part of every log drive. These one-man boats could easily be maneuvered around obstacles and would help rescue workers who had to get the key log out of a jam. Courtesy, The Muskegon Collection, Hackley Public Library

to move the logs down to Muskegon. Many boats followed the drive, small ones called "bateaux" and one large one called the "wangan." The bateaux had a number of uses such as a transport to and from the wangan, and as a "safety net" for the men breaking the log jams. The wangan carried two cooks who supplied all the meals. The thirty or so men on the drive ate four times a day—at 6:00 a.m., 10:00 a.m., 2:00 p.m., and 6:00 p.m. Bread was baked at night on the shore in front of a campfire.

The drive started when the ice melted in the spring. The men furthest upstream would roll their logs into the river and when these passed the next camp below, the men in this camp would follow suit, and so on down the river.

The most dangerous part of the drive occurred when a boulder or some other obstruction would cause the logs to jam; for miles back they would be stacked and tangled. When a jam occurred, the best drivers would look over the front of the jam to determine where the key log was. The key log was the log which, when loosened, would allow the other logs to follow. It was a very dangerous business. Sometimes the key log would have to be sawed and, in later years, even dynamited to clear a jam. The boss driver and one or two of his helpers would stay behind for the final clearing and then jump onto a bateaux, located just below the jam. Not all of them made it to safety.

Another problem was that rivers flooded bottomlands in the spring and many logs drifted away. Clearing these logs from the bottomlands and getting them back to the river was arduous labor.

There soon developed a difficulty in distinguishing who the

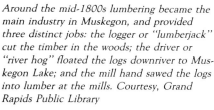

Around the mid-1800s lumbering became the main industry in Muskegon, and provided three distinct jobs: the logger or "lumberjack" cut the timber in the woods; the driver or "river hog" floated the logs downriver to Muskegon Lake; and the mill hand sawed the logs into lumber at the mills. Courtesy, Grand Rapids Public Library

With so many mills operating around Muskegon Lake, a method had to be devised to insure that each log got to the right mill. These are some common log marks of the mid-1870s. Courtesy, William J. Brinen Collection

logs belonged to. At first, the owner's mark was cut into the logs' sides with an ax. This meant that most marks were straight lines or "x's"—anything that could be cut easily with an ax. Side marking proved to be unsatisfactory because the logs frequently had to be turned, even though the marks were made on two sides. Owners began using marking hammers to make symbols or brands on the ends of logs. A colorful collection of logmarks resulted much like brands on horses and cattle.

This method of unorganized log driving continued until 1852 when the Log and Mill Owners Association was formed. A voluntary organization, it was paid for by assessment with each man paying according to the value of his logs. Major Chauncey Davis, Robert W. Morris, and John Ruddiman supervised the operation. Under this arrangement, the cost of driving logs was reduced to fifteen or twenty cents per thousand. The association was superseded by the Lumberman's Association in 1855.

An important court decision in an 1852 St. Clair County lawsuit had a great bearing on Muskegon's future in the lumbering business. The court held that as long as a stream had the capacity for floatage, it was navigable and all persons using it had equal rights. The decision assured lumbermen they could continue to float logs without interference from competitors or landowners along the river.

All timber along the Muskegon River from the mouth to Houghton Lake was thus available for cutting which catapulted Muskegon into the forefront of the lumber business.

MARTIN RYERSON: MUSKEGON'S FIRST MILLIONAIRE

Martin Ryerson walked to Muskegon from Grand Haven at age eighteen, where he made his fortune in just fifteen years. Courtesy, Grand Rapids Public Library

Muskegon produced some forty millionaires in its short but memorable lumber era and Martin Ryerson was the first. In fact, his was a true "rags-to-riches" story some fifteen years after having arrived in the area, almost penniless. Despite his many contributions to the county there is little to remember him by—the small and virtually insignificant Ryerson Creek, Ryerson Road near Twin Lake, and the Old Indian Cemetery, which was donated to Muskegon by his son.

The son of a poor farmer, Ryerson was born January 6, 1818, near Paterson, New Jersey. He had little schooling but was ambitious and, at the age of sixteen with a little money from his parents, he set out for the West. When he got as far as Detroit he was penniless but he found a job and earned enough to continue to Grand Rapids. He stopped there for more than a year doing odd jobs for the trader Louis Campeau, and Richard Godfrey. In May 1836, he walked to Muskegon by way of Grand Haven.

The story has it that Ryerson, who apparently struck out cross-country after going about halfway up the beach between Grand Haven and Muskegon, came to the Muskegon River where he encountered fur trader Joseph Troutier going up the river on a flatboat. Troutier, known as "Truckee," took the lad on board and they continued the trip to Maple Island where Troutier lived. As a result, Ryerson went to work for Troutier as a cook and chore boy at a wage said to be eight dollars a month.

Troutier was half Indian and his wife was a full-blooded Ottawa. A large colony of Indians lived around Muskegon Lake and Ryerson quickly learned the Ottawa language and adopted many Indian customs. He became a great favorite of the Indians and afterwards married a Chippewa woman living there. By reason of this marriage and his friendship with the Indians, Ryerson was able to purchase valuable timberland for very little and these investments yielded him handsome profits.

After about three years, Ryerson left the employ of Troutier and went to work for P.T. Newell, who came to Muskegon from Connecticut and opened a trading post in 1836. This employ marked the beginning of Ryerson's meteoric rise to wealth. While working for Newell, Ryerson lived with Louis Baddeaux, another early trader, and when Baddeaux died, Ryerson bought a farm sixteen miles up the Muskegon River. The first wagon in the area was made by Newell and Company and Ryerson bought it for his farm. He loaned it to his neighbors whenever they needed it.

By 1840 the supply of fur-bearing animals in the Muskegon area had become virtually exhausted, and Ryerson turned his interests to lumbering. In 1839 Newell and Company began construction of a sawmill on what is now Western Avenue between Pine and Spring, completing it the following year. In October 1841, Ryerson formed a partnership with S.J. Green, a newcomer, and they signed a contract with Newell to run the mill for two years. It was a modest mill by later standards, with one upright saw which could turn out about 50,000 board feet of lumber in a year. Its total cost was about four thousand dollars.

Green later dropped out of the business but Ryerson continued to manage the mill until 1845 when he went in with J.H. Knickerbocker and bought out his employer. Ryerson al-ways was considered the brains of the business and in the early years it is reported that he sometimes worked as much as eighteen hours a day, taking any job, no matter how difficult, that needed attention.

In 1847 Ryerson, at his own expense, built the first wagon road to Grand Rapids following an Indian trail that went through the present site of Ravenna. The usual route to Grand Rapids during that time was by foot along the beach to Grand Haven, and then by boat or stage the rest of the way.

Besides his position at the mill, Ryerson also served as clerk of Muskegon Township in 1842, receiving $3.52 for a year's salary. This paid for copying fourteen folios at thirteen cents each; the rest was his fee for attending one township meeting.

One daughter, Mary, was born of Ryerson's marriage to the Chippewa woman, whose name is not recorded. His first wife died shortly after the birth and he then married at Grand Haven the daughter of Pierre C. Duverney, a French-Canadian of great learning. This second Mrs. Ryerson died without bearing a child. He then married a daughter of Antoine Campeau of Grand Rapids. They had one child, Martin A. Ryerson, born in Chicago in 1857.

Ryerson left Muskegon for Chicago in 1851, apparently feeling that the big city offered more opportunities. He retained his interest in Muskegon, however, and accumulated a fortune of about four million dollars. He died in Boston in 1887.

Workers prepare to load a lumber schooner at the Ferry-Dowling Mill with the town of Montague in the background. This was in 1873, about twenty years before the lumber boom died in Muskegon County. Courtesy, Muskegon Chronicle

3 *The Lumber Queen*

In 1859 Muskegon was still a part of Ottawa County and supervisors worried that the area would soon be too large to govern. When Muskegon became a county in July 1859 it already had six townships and a seventh was added the day the new county was established. Muskegon County had by then a population of 3,947, according to the federal census. By 1864 it had grown to 5,500.

Creation of the new county may have relieved the Ottawa County supervisors of some problems but it presented some new ones to Muskegon. The first major decision was the location of the county seat. Just because Muskegon Township was the site of the county's first sawmill not everyone agreed it should be the seat of county government.

Businessmen and settlers of the White Lake area made attractive presentations to have the county seat located at Whitehall or Montague. It took ten years before the wrangle was settled and Muskegon was designated the county seat. By that time the county had a population of 14,804.

Muskegon Township became a village on July 8, 1861. The first election was held in the basement of the Methodist Episcopal Church; Lyman G. Mason was elected village president. In 1886 he also served as mayor of Muskegon, which was incorporated as a city by the state legislature in 1869. The new city earned the name "Lumber Queen" as lumbering continued on the rise. Forty-seven lumber mills, planing mills, and shingle mills soon surrounded Muskegon Lake.

But with the outbreak of the Civil War in 1861, much of this civic and business activity took second place. The county was not slow to answer President Abraham Lincoln's initial call for volunteers.

The first Muskegon unit to be organized was Company H of the Third Michigan Infantry. Its full complement of 100 men

Above: *Captain Jonathan Walker was buried in Muskegon's Evergreen Cemetery April 30, 1878. He was the only man ever convicted and sentenced to be branded by a federal court. Before the Civil War he carried the brand "S.S." (for "Slave Stealer") on the palm of his hand after helping seven runaway slaves board his vessel near Pensacola, Florida. The display of his branded hand during abolitionist rallies was said to be worth "a Union army corps." Courtesy, The Muskegon Collection, Hackley Public Library*

Right: *When Muskegon became a city in 1869 it needed a city hall; this ornate building was erected for that purpose in the 1880s. Note the fire bell in the top of the steeple. Courtesy, The Muskegon Collection, Hackley Public Library*

was recruited in a few days and enrolled May 13, 1861. Known as the Muskegon Rangers, they reportedly all were stalwart lumberjacks. These strapping men caused a sensation whenever they conducted close-order drills in Muskegon and later in Grand Rapids and Detroit. The company was under command of Captain Emery D. Bryant.

The regiment saw its first active service at Blackburn's Ford in northern Virginia. As part of the Army of the Potomac, the Third participated in every major battle—except the Battle of Antietam—until the Battle of Cold Harbor on June 9, 1864. In three years of service the Rangers lost thirty-one men and had nine desertions.

A second unit from Muskegon, Company E of the Second Michigan Cavalry, was organized by Ben Whitman who became its first captain. Recruitment was completed October 2, 1861, and the unit was sent to St. Louis where it was attached to the Army of the Cumberland. The company fought in a number of engagements in Mississippi, Tennessee, and Kentucky before ending its service in Alabama.

Above and Left: *Among the improvements in logging the woods was the introduction of oversized wheels, making it possible for logs to be chained underneath and then dragged by horse teams out of the woods. Courtesy, Muskegon Chronicle*

49

The third principal Muskegon unit was Company C of the Twenty-sixth Michigan Infantry organized in December 1862 with James A. Lathian its first captain. This unit served in most major battles near the end of the war including the final act, the surrender to Grant at Appomattox Court House, Virginia.

There was one other unit which contained a number of Muskegon men, Company F of the Fifth Michigan Cavalry. Mustered on August 30, 1862, the company was commanded by Captain Noah Ferry of Montague. Among the action seen by this company was Gettysburg, where Captain Ferry lost his life.

When the Rangers returned home, the first unit to arrive, they received a rousing welcome. Dump wagons, forty or more, came from the mills and a huge circular saw blade hung on each. As the parade, led by local attorney James F. Snow, headed into the business district, the saw blades were struck by mallets, making a terrific din. Snow reportedly made an imposing sight wearing a stovepipe hat astride a white mule. The parade made frequent stops at saloons and ended abruptly at Pine and Western when the mule was given some refreshment.

The celebrating at the end of the war was short-lived when the county learned of President Lincoln's assassination. He was very

popular in the region, having received large majorities in the elections of 1860 and 1864. Almost the total population went into deep mourning and a memorial service was held at the Methodist Episcopal Church.

*   *   *

The Civil War, nevertheless, had little effect on the growth of Muskegon's lumber industry. The day of the independent logger and his forty or eighty acres of timber faded with the introduction of large companies which bought timberland by the hundreds of acres. Booms were set up along the bottomlands of rivers to prevent logs from drifting away when the water was high. The size of the camps increased from eight men to somewhere between fifty to a hundred.

In many places the railroad replaced the horse and ox to get logs to the river so that mills could operate almost year-round. Winfield Scott Gerrish of Muskegon is credited with introducing the logging railroad. Most people, including his father, thought his idea was crazy but Gerrish had noticed railroad features at the Philadelphia Centennial that he thought would make logging

Below: *This is the Matthew Wilson Company sawmill on Muskegon Lake during the 1880s. The continuous chain at the right pulled logs up the incline to the saws located on the second floor. The silo-like chimney at the left—which burned slag and bark—was covered with a wire mesh so that sparks could not escape. Courtesy, William J. Brinen Collection*

Opposite page, top and bottom: *Winfield Scott Gerrish of Muskegon is credited with inventing the logging railroad in the late 1870s. He built the rails from the river to the cuts, enabling the transport of logs to the river year-round and assuring a continual supply of logs to the mills. Top picture courtesy, The Muskegon Collection, Hackley Public Library. Bottom picture courtesy, William J. Brinen Collection*

trains possible. Gerrish built his railroad from the river to the timber and within a few years the railroad became a fixture in the woods.

Noticeable improvements took place in the mill. The rapid circular saw and huge gang saws replaced the mulay or single-sash saw. Steam eliminated man or animal power to lift logs up to the saw. Conveyor chains and movable platforms added to the output. In 1860 one man was employed for every 1,000 feet of finished lumber. Improvements soon altered this to one man for every 3,000 feet sawed. Many tools were invented in Muskegon and some are still used in the lumbering industry.

For some thirty years Muskegon rode a wave of prosperity with money flowing into the city. At its peak Muskegon had forty millionaires and more money and silk hats per capita than anywhere in the United States.

Most of the mill owners lived like kings. They built palatial residences and their wives wore expensive imported gowns. Muskegon's sawdust streets saw the handsomest carriages and best

Below: *The Davies Iron Works on Western Avenue between Fourth and Fifth was established by Joshua Davies in 1858. All kinds of sawmill machinery were made and repaired there as displayed in this 1874 photo. Courtesy, Charles H. Yates Collection, Muskegon County Museum*

Opposite page, top: *One of the elaborate homes owned by Muskegon's elite during the lumber boom was Lyman G. Mason's. Once the old Union School, as Mason's home it contained thirty rooms and eight fireplaces. In 1903 the Sisters of Mercy bought the Mason house and grounds and it became the first Mercy Hospital. Courtesy, The Muskegon Collection, Hackley Public Library*

Opposite page, bottom: *Matthew Wilson owned this home, located at Muskegon and Pine. Razed by the Pine Street Fire in 1891, the county built a jail on the property in 1892. The jail later became the home of the Muskegon County Museum. Courtesy, The Muskegon Collection, Hackley Public Library*

horses in the world. Lavish entertainment was the vogue with mill owners vying with each other in displaying their riches.

As timber fell to support the mill owners' extravagant life-styles, a chronicler of the day wrote: "There is nothing improbable in the prediction that under favorable auspices the city of Muskegon will cut a billion feet of lumber annually." (One billion feet of lumber could house a population of 125,000 or build a board highway across the continent.) But Muskegon never produced that volume: the peak in 1887 was slightly less than half of this prediction.

Such enormous wealth produced yet another institution— banking. In 1859 Captain Thomas J. Rand, who had a varied career as a sailor, a merchant, and in other businesses, formed an alliance with the private banking firm of Daniel Ball & Company of Grand Rapids. He established a branch bank in Muskegon which thirteen years later developed into Lumberman's National Bank and is now FMB Lumberman's Bank.

Most of the banking business in those early lumbering days was with mill owners rather than private individuals. Logs and

Above: *This is how the Muskegon River looked in the spring of 1887—the peak year for logging in Muskegon. It was said a person could walk for miles on the river and never get his feet wet. Courtesy, The Muskegon Collection, Hackley Public Library*

Opposite page, top: *The Thayer Lumber Company mill was one of Muskegon's top producers during the lumber boom. This 1888 photo shows the huge piles of lumber in front of the mill. Courtesy, The Muskegon Collection, Hackley Public Library*

Opposite page, bottom: *The bateaux crew in 1888 was photographed during the biggest drive on the Muskegon River. The picture was taken near Newaygo. A wangan, or cook's boat, is in the background. Courtesy, William J. Brinen Collection*

MUSKEGON LOG BOOMING COMPANY

Muskegon was the largest center of lumbering on lower Michigan's west coast. From the 1850's to the 1890's an immense amount of timber was floated to this port down the Muskegon River and its tributaries. In 1864 the Muskegon Booming Co. was formed to sort the logs and raft them to the mills. Here at the upper end of Muskegon Lake was the great storage boom where the logs, each identified by its owner's log mark, were sorted into pens as fast as they floated in. They were then chained together into rafts which were towed to the mills by the company's tugboats. In thirty years the company delivered over ten billion board feet of logs.

Above: *All that remains of Muskegon's great lumber era is this historical marker located in Richard's Park at the end of Ottawa Street. It marks the site of the Muskegon Booming Company's sorting pens where logs were collected for transportation to their proper mills. Photo by Dave Carlson. Courtesy, Dave Carlson*

Right: *Major Chauncey Davis was Muskegon's first mayor in 1869. He was also the first president of the Muskegon Booming Company in 1864. Both in 1860 and 1864 he represented the district in the state legislature. Courtesy, The Muskegon Collection, Hackley Public Library*

lumber were safe collateral. Once the logs were measured and in the rollways for their trip downriver, lumbermen could get advances from bankers by carrying their property as collateral. This made the Rand Bank a wonderful convenience to men engaged in the expanding lumber business. Until 1867 Rand conducted his banking business assisted only by his wife.

More loggers meant more logs coming down the Muskegon River and for miles the waterway was solid with logs from bank to bank. The Muskegon Booming Company was formed in 1864 to bring some order to the chaos of getting the right logs to the right mills. The booming company floated logs down the river to Muskegon Lake into sorting yards where they were separated and delivered to the proper mill. In its first year the company handled 96,045,814 feet of logs; in 1881 the amount of lumber handled had climbed to 565,846,557 feet. The company thus became one of the area's biggest employers.

The booming company men, armed with pike poles (long poles with a metal point on the end) separated the logs by log marks into groups. These were gathered together and towed to the proper mills by tugs and small steamboats.

The Lake Harbor Hotel on Mona Lake was one of the Muskegon area's best known resorts shortly after World War I. It was destroyed by fire in the mid-1920s. Courtesy, Manistee County Museum

Only one of these two famous Muskegon landmarks survive. Hackley Park in the foreground still exists but the Occidental Hotel (left) was razed for a parking lot for the Muskegon Mall in 1976. Courtesy, Manistee County Museum

Above: *Lake Michigan Park was a popular recreation center for Muskegonites in the early part of the twentieth century. The Muskegon Traction and Light Company made connections with the park by streetcar and the facilities were used for swimming, concerts, plays and eating. Courtesy, The Gillette Nature Center*

Opposite page, top: *Lake Michigan's beaches have always been one of Muskegon's great natural assets. The only change over the years has been the costumes. This is a scene near the old Lake Michigan Park about seventy-five years ago. Courtesy, The Gillette Nature Center*

Opposite page, bottom: *The old float bridge over Mona Lake could be swung out to enable boats to pass. It has long since been replaced by a modern structure. Courtesy, Collection of Leslie Ruth Chase*

Opposite page, top: *The Walter Duke lumber camp was typical of many in the late 1800s. It stood near Fruitvale and Sand Creek. Shown from left: the blacksmith shop with shaving bench and grindstone; the bunkhouse in the background; and across the road, the barn. Courtesy, White Lake Chamber of Commerce*

Opposite page, bottom: *Through summer and fall as trees were cut and felled, they were piled on roadside "skidways" to be loaded on sleds and hauled to rollways in the winter. The straight, free-standing trees were cut away first to expose dangerous leaning trees, or "widow-makers," which were felled. Courtesy, White Lake Chamber of Commerce*

Above: *Whitehall artist Frederick Norman was commissioned for a series of paintings depicting lumbering. Here, this load of logs is on its way from the woods to the rollway. Courtesy, White Lake Chamber of Commerce*

Left: *This Norman painting, High Rollway, is of the White River's South Branch. The riverman is attaching a line to the key log, to be pulled out by oxen on the opposite bank, releasing the entire pile of logs to roll into the water. Courtesy, White Lake Chamber of Commerce*

Top: *River jams were frequent during the driving season, especially if logs were not driven out during the spring "rise." This scene was probably composed from sketches made on the White River's North Branch. Courtesy, White Lake Chamber of Commerce*

Above: *Just above the present railroad in Whitehall were the White River "booming grounds." Here the logs driven downstream were sorted by "log works" for cutting at the various mills. Courtesy, White Lake Chamber of Commerce*

Above: *Finally, the last stop for the logs was the mill, such as this Staples & Covell mill, which enjoyed the greatest and most enduring success of all the White Lake mills. Courtesy, White Lake Chamber of Commerce*

Left: *From the mills, ships took the lumber to Chicago and other markets. Muskegon's harbor was rated one of the finest on the Great Lakes, as it daily received passenger and freight vessels. Courtesy, Manistee County Museum*

The Muskegon Booming Company's sorting grounds were located at the upper end of Muskegon Lake. Here logs were sorted into pens, according to their log marks, then rafted and towed to the various mills by tugs or small steamboats. Courtesy, The Muskegon Collection, Hackley Public Library

As one might suspect there was talk of log piracy and undoubtedly it did occur. The pirate only needed to saw a few inches off the log's end where the mark appeared and hammer in a new one. Large scale piracy, however, would have been close to impossible. The job would have to be done at night, logs would have to be hauled onto the riverbank in the dark, and wet, sixteen-foot logs would have to be wrestled with in the mud. At best it would have been a most hazardous undertaking.

*   *   *

While logs rolled down the river, Muskegon residents dreamt of trains rolling through town. In addition to being the first president of Muskegon village, Lyman G. Mason also was a sawmill owner and operator, a realtor and developer, politician, banker, and civic leader. One of his most important contributions to Muskegon was the building of its railroads.

In 1860 Mason helped organize Muskegon & Ferrysburg Railroad Company, which was formed to build a railroad to Ferrysburg, the nearest station of the Detroit & Milwaukee Railway. He was the first president of the company and served in that capacity until the railroad merged with the Allegan & Grand Haven.

Above: *The old swing bridge that linked Montague and Whitehall was built in 1864. It was called a "swing" bridge because it turned halfway around to allow tugs to go up to the booming grounds. Courtesy, Muskegon Chronicle*

Opposite page, top: *This is White River at Old Channel Trail about 1867. Note the spectators who wished to be photographed standing on the roofs of stores and buildings. Courtesy, Muskegon Chronicle*

Opposite page, bottom: *The first float bridge over Mona Lake was built in 1879 and had a section in the middle that swung open so boats could pass. This picture, taken in the late 1880s, shows the Thomas Hume family in the buggy. The bridge was replaced in 1909. Courtesy, Charles H. Yates Collection, Muskegon County Museum*

In 1872 Mason proposed building a railroad from Muskegon to Big Rapids to develop and promote lumber interests in the Muskegon River valley. The Muskegon & Big Rapids Railroad Company was duly organized with Mason as president. He also took a prominent role in the building of a branch of the Grand Rapids & Indiana Railroad to Muskegon. It was largely through his influence that Muskegon secured another important railroad, the Toledo, Saginaw and Muskegon, which eventually became part of the Grand Trunk system.

Through Mason's friendly relationship with Captain A.E. Goodrich, Muskegon became linked with Chicago on the daily line of sidewheel steamers in 1862. In 1864 he led the move to improve Muskegon's harbor at a cost of $50,000, raised by lumbermen and businessmen.

The Goodrich Company steamer *Alpena* turned out to be one of the Great Lakes' greatest shipping disasters. It left Muskegon

Immense piles of lumber circled Muskegon Lake awaiting shipment to Chicago. This is a view at Lakeside in 1888 with several mills in the background. Courtesy, The Muskegon Collection, Hackley Public Library

at 3:30 p.m. Friday, October 16, 1880, and then from Grand Haven at 8:00 p.m. with seventy-five passengers and a crew of twenty-six bound for Chicago. Although Lake Michigan was calm, the light keeper at Grand Haven informed Captain Napier of the *Alpena* that a heavy storm would strike soon. The captain said he would be nearly across the lake by the time it struck and started off for Chicago.

The worst storm in Lake Michigan history, up to that time, struck about midnight. Anxiety began to build in Muskegon when there was no word from the *Alpena.* On Monday a section of the cabin and various articles with the *Alpena*'s name on them were found on the beach between Grand Haven and Holland. A few bodies and debris subsequently washed ashore; it was surmised that the ship had gone down about thirty miles off Holland. Some of the splintered wood indicated an explosion. As the tragedy became apparent, the beach was regularly patrolled

The Carrie A. Ryerson *steamer carried passengers and freight from Muskegon to Bay Mill. She was built in 1883 and sold to Thomas Young of Chicago in 1910. The ship burned at Willow Springs, Illinois, in 1921. Courtesy, William J. Brinen Collection*

but only six bodies were found. Two messages, one scratched on the bottom of a grape basket, the other on a shingle and signed by the captain, indicated the *Alpena* was breaking apart but there never was any account of the actual unfolding of the disaster.

A coroner's jury convened at Grand Haven on January 2, 1881. It held that from the evidence presented, the *Alpena* was not seaworthy, that the crew was new and inexperienced—except for the captain and engineer—that life preservers were rotten and unfit for use, and that the one lifeboat they found was not seaworthy. The jury found the Goodrich company liable for loss of life and damages; Captain Goodrich was so angered over the decision that he suspended service on the Muskegon-Grand Haven-Chicago route for the 1881 season.

*　　*　　*

Another disaster of great proportion was the great Muskegon fire of August 1, 1874. Portions of twelve city blocks containing 300 buildings, 75 of them businesses, were destroyed. A total of thirty-six acres in the heart of the city were burned. The fire apparently started when an employee of a small circus visiting the city set fire to a barrel of wastepaper under a building stairway at the corner of Terrace and Western, in the main business district.

Fire prevention and fire fighting was of great concern to village and city fathers since the first mill was established. Residents lived with a constant threat of fire. Many mills were destroyed and fire was an ever-present danger. In these early days, occupants of every dwelling, shop, and mill were required to keep on hand one two-gallon bucket or pail for every able-bodied male between the ages of fifteen and fifty. When a fire alarm sounded, every male was required to go with his bucket to the scene of the fire. Bucket brigades were then formed from Muskegon Lake to the fire.

This primitive method proved unsatisfactory and, around 1870, the village council placed four reservoirs at strategic points near the business district. Each reservoir had three wood tanks. One tank held 35,000 gallons of water and the other two at least 25,000 gallons each. But this reservoir system just could not provide enough water, and so was of little help, in the 1874 fire.

By 1880 the city had five hose companies, manned by men who served as "horses," and one hook and ladder pulled by horses. The fire department was horse drawn until the conversion to motors began in 1916. The fire horse finally went out of commission in 1924.

Above: *Packers in Muskegon shingle mills were paid in shingle checks. Shingle packers received seven cents per thousand shingles and the average worker could pack 35,000 to 40,000 shingles a day. Courtesy,* Muskegon Chronicle

Top: *These men are using special saws and equipment to make shingles. Sawmill employees worked twelve-hour shifts a day. Courtesy,* Muskegon Chronicle

In the heyday of the lumber era (1881-1887) some 5,000 men were employed by the mills. Hundreds more worked in the bush or for the booming company. Most earned one dollar to $1.50 a day. Sawmill and boom company employees worked twelve hours a day. The mills worked two twelve-hour shifts to turn out the millions of board feet of lumber that were building the Midwest. Laborers who packed shingles received seven cents per thousand and the average worker could pack about 35,000 to 40,000 a day. Especially skilled workers could pack as many as 50,000. Booming company employees on the drive earned $1.50 a day if they stayed until the drive was finished. If they quit before that they received only $1.25 a day.

Early in 1881 men working for the boom company and the mills began agitating for shorter hours. The slogan "Ten Hours or No Sawdust" from the millhands and "Ten Hours or No Logs" from the rivermen became the watchwords for Muskegon's first labor strike. The strikers each paid twenty-five-cents dues to their "union" to finance the strike. By October only sixteen mills were operating ten hours, seven were operating eleven hours, and the remainder were closed down. After a relatively quiet winter, the strike resumed in the spring joined by the boom company employees.

The strike finally ended May 29, 1882, with a compromise. Most of the men went back to an eleven-hour schedule in the mills, working from 6:00 a.m. to 6:00 p.m. with an hour off for lunch, except for Saturdays when they quit at 5:00.

One of the strike leaders, William H. Wells—who died in Holton in 1929 at the age of ninety—claimed to have originated the "Ten Hours or No Sawdust" slogan. For his trouble he was blackballed in every mill in Muskegon and never again worked as a millhand after the strike.

TIMES WERE WILD WHEN LUMBERJACKS HIT TOWN

While the lumbering era generally brought prosperity to the Muskegon area, it also brought some wild goings-on, particularly in the spring.

This was the time when the drivers or river hogs came down the Muskegon River with the logs and pockets full of money to spend. Saloons and brothels, of which there were plenty, were the targets of these men and most certainly women, children, and respectable citizens kept off the streets while the celebrating lasted.

Much of the excitement took place on Ottawa Street, although there were an estimated sixty to eighty-five saloons in the city area. Most of them contained dance floors and long bars on the main floors while upstairs were rooms where the "ladies of the evening" plied their trade.

The most famous place of all was the Canterbury House on Marquette, located on top of what was called the Newaygo hill, on the road to Newaygo. Two blocks away from Getty Street in those days was the "boondocks," far away from the activity of a bustling lumber city and away from the restraints of local ordinances.

The house was supposedly built by Nan Jones in the middle 1870s. Very little is known about Ms. Jones. One must suspect, however, that she had a nose for money.

The Canterbury House reportedly was the scene of many a brawl that sometimes ended in killings. However, a close inspection of the records fail to document any murders. A former real estate agent, William Sharrock, who owned the house after 1914, reportedly dug several pounds of lead bullets out of the walls.

The original building consisted of a big dance hall with a high ceiling, a stage and a place for an orchestra, a bar room, and some thirty-six rooms on the second floor. The dance

floor had to be replaced many times since the lumberjacks came to town still wearing their spiked boots, or "caulks," used to maintain balance while riding on a log down the river. Regular dances used to be varied with prizefights and cockfights. Two walls formed part of the ring for a prizefight while ropes were stretched across the other part of the ring. The birds wore spurs in cockfights when the promotors were able to evade the law.

There were many impromptu fights, some extremely violent, when the "Jacks" would argue about the choice of partners for a square dance. Yet these fights never resulted in shootings, according to Napolean Belfy, one of Muskegon's early fire chiefs.

George Jones was employed by a livery stable as a fifteen-year-old and frequently drove customers to the Canterbury House in its heyday. He reports Mollie Gard and Jennie Morgan ran the place at separate times during its notoriety. During this time, John Williams, a wholesale

liquor dealer with a warehouse on Ottawa Street, owned the place and it served as a ready outlet for much of his liquor.

Many old-time Muskegon residents know the Canterbury House as a dairy farm owned by a Mrs. Anna Brusted before Sharrock purchased it in 1914 from Charles Gunn. Sharrock and his family lived in the place for four years; during that time the building was dismantled in pieces, with two sections moved to become separate homes. The rest was finally razed in 1934.

Undoubtedly the Canterbury House had something to do with a moniker for the Jackson Hill district which still holds today. Frequently the district is referred to as "Killgrubbin." The name supposedly originated from some popular belief that murders had been committed out in the surrounding wild woods. But there is still little reason to believe the rumors had any basis in fact.

A house of prostitution during the booming lumber days, the Ashley Furman house at the corner of Market and Terrace was built in the 1860s and razed in 1939. It also once served as a boardinghouse. Courtesy, Charles H. Yates Collection, Muskegon County Museum

The J.W. Miller Hardware Store on East Western near Pine was typical of Muskegon's downtown stores in 1880. Mr. Hofstra, the manager, is in the derby hat and shirtsleeves. Courtesy, Charles H. Yates Collection, Muskegon County Museum

4 *After the Lumber*

As the 1890s approached, Muskegon village had grown into a city of about 26,000 people; by 1890, the county boasted a population of over 40,000. The city had five wards with two supervisors from each. The city limits extended from Muskegon Lake to Laketon Avenue on the south, Getty Street on the east to the intersection of Laketon and Lakeshore Drive on the west. In 1889 Lakeside, including Bluffton and Port Sherman, was annexed. Rated the fifth city in Michigan in size and importance, three railroads served the metropolis, and there was daily boat service to Chicago.

Each township had its own civic services. The city's police department had a chief, an assistant chief, and twelve patrolmen. Meanwhile the fire department consisted of a chief, four hose companies, a hook and ladder truck, a steam fire engine, and twenty-six men. There were three national banks, one savings bank, a high school, and eight public school buildings with an administrator and eighty-six teachers. There were two Catholic parochial schools, three Catholic churches, and fourteen Protestant churches.

Whitehall and Montague, in the White Lake area, continued to grow with each nearing a population of 3,000. Both towns had their own police and fire departments and a railroad line north from Muskegon had been established.

Schools first appeared in the White Lake area in the 1850s with the public school system starting in the next decade.

Deacon Abner Bennett, an escaped slave who came to the area from Canada, brought organized religion to White Lake in 1853. He was a licensed Methodist exhorter for thirty-nine years until his death in 1879 at the age of eighty. The Presbyterian Church was organized in 1868 and became the Ferry Memorial Reformed Church in 1947. In the latter part of the nineteenth century, Catholic, Lutheran and Episcopal churches were established at White Lake.

Opposite page: *Until July 13, 1913 an airplane had never been seen in Muskegon's skies. While competing in a race from Chicago to Detroit, pioneer pilot Glenn Martin was forced down on the shores of Lake Michigan. After repairs, Martin flew over Muskegon Lake; the flight was watched by hundreds of spectators from the Muskegon Country Club grounds. The Theatrical Colony Yacht Club (now the Muskegon Yacht Club) is in the left background. Courtesy, Charles H. Yates Collection, Muskegon County Museum.*

Right: *The personnel of Muskegon Fire Department's Engine House No. 1 pose with their mascot in 1892. The firehouse was located at the old city hall on Jefferson Street. Courtesy, William J. Brinen Collection, Hackley Public Library*

Below: *By 1916 Muskegon had its first motorized fire equipment. Captain John Gannon is seated next to the driver. Courtesy, Charles H. Yates Collection, Muskegon County Museum*

The improvement of the causeway north of Muskegon eventually brought a road as well as the railroad line and travel by stage or private carriage was popular in the county.

Yet all this development would soon be interrupted. Only a few observers in the mid-1880s forecast that the county's life-blood, the lumbering industry, would be coming to an abrupt halt, when there were just no pines left to chop down. All the man in the street saw was the continuing parade of logs down the Muskegon and White rivers, the whir of saws in the mills ringing Muskegon and White lakes, and the glow in the night sky from burning sawdust and slag.

In 1887 a whopping 570,000,000 feet of lumber was cut; but this number proved to be the industry's apex which soon exhausted itself. The last mill, the Gow and Campbell in North Muskegon, closed down in 1910. Two years later James Gow bought out his partner and for a brief time cut lumber from logs salvaged from the bottom of the Muskegon river and lake.

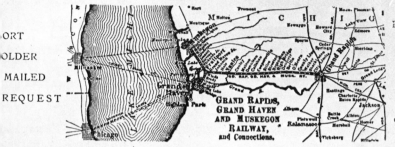

GRAND RAPIDS, GRAND HAVEN & MUSKEGON RY.

Connecting the Cities of

Muskegon   Grand Rapids   Grand Haven

FIRST CLASS THIRD RAIL INTERURBAN

32 TRIANS DAILY

ting the
ts on Muskegon Lake, Spring Lake, Lake Harbor, Lake Michigan

ORT

OLDER

MAILED

REQUEST

FAST FREIGHT
SERVICE

GRAND RAPIDS,
GRAND HAVEN
AND MUSKEGON
RAILWAY,
and Connections.

S. L. VAUGHAN
Traffic Manager
GRAND RAPIDS, MICH.

Left and below: *One of the Muskegon area's most popular forms of public transportation after the turn of the century was the Grand Rapids, Grand Haven & Muskegon Railway, or the Interurban as it was popularly known, which connected the three cities. In operation from 1902 to 1926, it did much to develop the resort business and greatly improved freight and passenger service between Muskegon and Grand Rapids. Courtesy, The Muskegon Collection, Hackley Public Library*

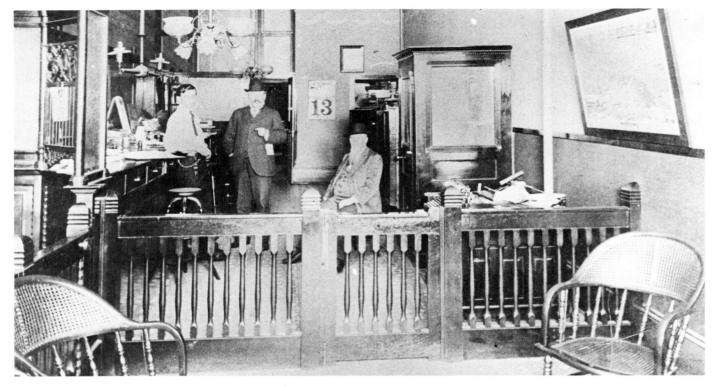

Above: *One of the great lumber alliances in Muskegon was between Charles H. Hackley and Thomas Hume. This is a photo of their office located on the north side of Western Avenue between Second and Third streets. From left to right are Thomas Hume's son George, Thomas Hume, and Charles H. Hackley. Courtesy, The Muskegon Collection, Hackley Public Library*

Left: *The first of Charles H. Hackley's many gifts to Muskegon was Hackley Public Library. Thousands attended the dedication ceremonies May 24, 1888. The date is remembered every year by Muskegon public school students who get a half-day off. Courtesy, The Muskegon Collection, Hackley Public Library*

Opposite page, top: *This 1888 photograph shows how Hackley Park appeared before Charles H. Hackley bought the land and then donated the property to the city. The old Central School appears in the right background and Hackley Library is in the left. Courtesy, Charles H. Yates Collection, Muskegon County Museum*

Opposite page, bottom: *Charles H. Hackley greatly helped Muskegon recover after the lumber industry collapsed. While most lumber barons "took the money and ran," Hackley returned millions to the city where he made his fortune. Courtesy, The Muskegon Collection, Hackley Public Library*

Muskegon's city population dropped from 26,000 to 16,000 as millworkers and others connected with the lumber industry moved west, attracted by new forests. Mills were dismantled and their machinery also moved west. Many downtown businesses were abandoned and boarded up. The city looked like a ghost town.

But all was not lost. A group of millionaire lumbermen stayed behind to help the city recover. Foremost of these was Charles H. Hackley whose name is more closely linked with Muskegon than any other individual. He came to Muskegon City at nineteen and got a job in the Durckee, Truesdell & Company mill. In a few years he was part-owner of the Hackley & Hume Company mill and later went on to become a true lumber "baron." He made most of his money in the purchase of vast timberland along the Muskegon River and later in other states and Canada. While most of the lumber barons "took the money and ran," Hackley returned many millions to the city where he had made his fortune.

Hackley's gifts, including endowments after his death, totaled about six million dollars and it would take close to seventy million dollars to replace them today. They include Hackley Public Library, Hackley Park and its five statues, Hackley School, and Hackley Manual Training School. He also contributed Hackley Hospital, Hackley Art Gallery (now Muskegon Museum of Art),

Opposite page, top and bottom: *Charles H. Hackley's gifts to Muskegon also included the Hackley Manual Training School (top) in 1897, one of the first schools in the country devoted exclusively to manual training. Bottom: Hackley Hospital, circa 1920. This photograph shows the buildings much as they looked originally; they have all since been replaced. Courtesy, The Muskegon Collection, Hackley Public Library.*

Below: *One of Muskegon's diversified industries established after the lumber era was the Muskegon Brewery, built in 1884. Note the wooden street and streetcar tracks in this 1900 photo. Courtesy, Charles H. Yates Collection, Muskegon's County Museum*

the Julia E. Hackley Poor Fund, the Muskegon Humane Endowment (now the Muskegon Children's Home), and the Julia E. Hackley Educational Fund. This final endowment was from the remainder of Hackley's estate; it was bequeathed in his wife's will to the Muskegon Board of Education, for the development of educational projects. This fund alone amounted to $1,948,218.

Other reminders of Charles Hackley in Muskegon City are a street and high school athletic field, both named after him. His home, considered a model in Victorian architecture and under restoration since 1970, includes many of the original furnishings. Muskegon public school students still pay tribute to Hackley every May 25, Hackley Day. After morning programs outline Hackley's gifts to the city, the schools are then dismissed for the day.

As is frequently the case with the wealthy, there has been some questioning of Hackley's motives for all his largesse. One theory maintains Hackley hoped the city's name would be changed to Hackleyville if he contributed enough. But this hardly seems plausible, considering that Hackley was shy and retiring to a fault. When called upon to speak at the dedication of Hackley Park on May 30, 1900, he stood and said: "Ladies and gentle-

The Julius Loescher & Son Tannery located on Lakeshore Drive was the first firm brought here by the Bonus Fund, established by the Muskegon Chamber of Commerce to attract new industries to replace the lumber industry. It was in business from 1895 until 1934. Courtesy, Charles H. Yates Collection, Muskegon County Museum

men, I never made a speech in my life and I never expect to make one, but I will call upon my friend, Mr. Temple, to help me." By prearrangement Ansel F. Temple, mayor of Muskegon from 1897 to 1898—while plans for the park statues were being finalized—filled in for Hackley.

A better explanation for Hackley's generosity is that he believed Muskegon should be a quality city, and thus attract new business and industry to replace the departed lumber boom. Many of the new businesses appropriately enough carried the Hackley name, as well as those of ex-lumbermen Thomas Hume, Newcomb McGraft, and other civic leaders who stayed in the board of directors roster.

Hackley and his group of community leaders concluded that Muskegon County must obtain diversified industries to replace the lumber industry. Muskegon was bonded for $200,000 for "park and wharfage purposes"—a subterfuge to market the bonds and circumvent any legal obstacles. Actually, the money would be used as a factory fund for the city.

This factory fund supported three "bonus plans"—in 1893, 1903, and 1910. There were several methods of determining the

Muskegon's first streetcars were horse or mule drawn on three-and-a-half miles of track. This 1890 photo shows a car on Brewery Hill. Mules were used in the summer and horses in the winter; they were replaced by electric cars after 1890. Courtesy, Charles H. Yates Collection, Muskegon County Museum

amount of bonus to be paid. The most common way, a new company was allowed $100 for each person it expected to employ. The bonus was paid in exchange for a mortgage on the factory. The mortgage was then cancelled if after seven years of operation the average number of employees equalled or exceeded the estimated number. If the average employment number could not be maintained, the company was asked to return a proportionate amount of the bonus. If a company failed, the chamber of commerce took over the plant and tried to sell it to a new company.

Besides these bonuses, companies could acquire loans from the fund, with a straight pay-back arrangement. Fund money also subsidized construction costs for a new company.

Voters approved the first bond issue in 1893, by a vote of 2,093 to 367. Central Paper Company—now the S.D. Warren Division of Scott Paper Company—and Shaw-Walker remain major companies today of the firms brought here by this first bonus fund.

In 1903 however, the fund was depleted and the city again bonded itself for $100,000. This time the supposed bond issue

Opposite page, top: *Continental Motor Manufacturing was one of the industries brought here by Muskegon's second Bonus Fund of 1903. It survives today as Teledyne Continental Motors. The plant pictured in this 1915 photograph was torn down and the entire operation moved to Getty Street. In the right corner is the original 1906 building. Courtesy, Charles H. Yates Collection, Muskegon County Museum*

Opposite page, bottom: *One of the seven original industries started in Muskegon Heights after the lumber boom died was the Standard Malleable Iron Works Company, located at Sanford and Sherman. It was started in 1896; later the building became part of Norge. Courtesy, Charles H. Yates Collection, Muskegon County Museum*

was for construction of a municipal wharf. The vote was 1,206 to 83 in favor. Continental Motor Manufacturing Company was brought to Muskegon in 1906 through the industrial recruiting efforts of the Muskegon Chamber of Commerce. For fifty years it was the county's largest employer. Brunswick Balke-Collender received one of the largest bonuses ever—$50,000 for guaranteeing employment of 500 workers. Both companies are still operating today in Muskegon: Continental is now two separate companies— General and Industrial Products, Teledyne Continental Motors, divisions of Teledyne Industries, Inc.

A somewhat similar plan was being followed south of Muskegon village, in what became Muskegon Heights. A syndicate of Muskegon businessmen organized the Muskegon Improvement Company, in 1888, with Lyman G. Mason as president. One year later the company received title to about 1,000 acres of land. Seven industries were under contract to move to Muskegon Heights from nearby states, if the sale of lots was successful. By 1890 the territory was platted with ten acres reserved for a park site—where Muskegon Heights High School now stands—and 110 acres reserved for factory sites. The rest of the acreage was reserved for housing developments.

On May 12, 1890, 2,888 Muskegon Heights lots were sold in a giant lottery for a total of $364,000 at $130 for a 50 by 125 foot lot. It wasn't until five months later that purchasers learned where their property was located and who their neighbors were going to be. That September there was a subsequent sale of 2,000 lots at $165 each. The final sale of lots several years later included homes and lots valued from $1,000 to $5,000 each.

The seven original Muskegon Heights' industries were: Alaska Refrigeration Company, Morton Manufacturing Company, Standard Malleable Iron Works, Kelley Brothers Manufacturing Company, Nelson Piano Company, Gray Brothers Manufacturing Company, and Shaw Crane Works. Of these seven, Shaw Crane is the only survivor today, as Dresser Crane & Hoist, of Dresser Industries, Inc.

Muskegon Heights became a village June 2, 1891, with a population of about 800. At the time of the Panic of 1893 there were thirteen industries and about 1,300 people in Muskegon Heights. Only four industries survived—Michigan Washing Machine, Morton Manufacturing, Alaska Refrigeration, and Shaw Crane. Many people lost their lots because of not paying their taxes. But Muskegon Heights survived; it became a city July 16, 1902 and today is an integral part of the county.

Like Muskegon Heights, North Muskegon became a village in 1891 and also experienced some very difficult times. North Mus-

Above: *This 1900 photograph shows Whitehall as a village, looking east on Colby Street. Courtesy,* Muskegon Chronicle

Above, left: *In 1915 the Muskegon Heights Bus Company put a bus in operation since the streetcars could not reach all areas. This bus, called a jitney, is shown on Peck Street in front of Marsh Field. Courtesy; Charles H. Yates Collection, Muskegon County Museum*

kegon could not become an industrialized suburb of Muskegon because there was no rail transportation available. In fact the only way to reach North Muskegon from Muskegon was to travel across the ice in winter, ride a boat in the summer, or take the causeway, which in those days was a very rough road made up of slag from the mills, broken canoes, and anything else available: it had to be replaced frequently.

Nevertheless, North Muskegon survived as a resort setting and now is a bedroom community containing many of the area's professional and industrial leaders.

Developments in the White Lake area of the county after the lumbering boom were similar to those in North Muskegon. The Muskegon River made transportation difficult to the north, thus slowing industrial growth. The White Lake area, like North Muskegon, then turned to tourism as a primary economic source.

*　　　*　　　*

Only seventeen years after the fire of 1874 came the Great Fire of 1891 (also known as the Pine Street Fire). The day, May 16, started off pleasantly. Fire Chief J.K. Fallon was standing in the doorway of the No. 3 fire station when an alarm was telephoned to the No. 1 station at 2:00 p.m. The caller reported, "There is a little fire near the barn at the Lankwell house. Please send the [fire extinguishing] chemical." Chief Fallon dispatched the No. 3 company and, as he was making the run, turned in a general alarm.

Top, right: *The bottom floor of Tubby's Block on the northeast corner of Pine and Walton was occupied in 1888 by the Castenholz Meat Market. The meat available included pork, venison, and various domestic and game birds. This building was also destroyed in the Pine Street Fire of May 16, 1891. Courtesy, Charles H. Yates Collection, Muskegon County Museum*

The fire was in the Hampshire barn of the Lankwell home on Clay Avenue and was much larger than the caller had indicated. It ate its way down Pine Street to the John Hamilton house on Iona Street before it was finally checked, covering a total distance of seventeen acres. A total of 250 homes and businesses in a seventeen-acre area was laid to waste. Even the courthouse, which had escaped the 1874 fire, was destroyed. Firemen did not suffer so much from a water shortage as they had in 1874, but with strong breezes fanning the flames in tinder-dry wooden buildings, the firefighters had little chance to stem the tide.

But Muskegon Township was not long in rebuilding. The board of supervisors met on May 18 to begin plans for a new courthouse; by 1892 it was opened. The lumbermen, bankers, and other well-to-do built new homes. The workers and small businessmen rebuilt also. Some had temporary stores ready in just a few days.

Like Muskegon, Whitehall was visited by two substantial fires. The first took place July 30, 1881; the second happened just nine years later.

The first inferno was the biggest and most devastating. It was discovered about 2:00 a.m. by a watchman at the Linderman mill who observed flames in the vicinity of Sturtevant's livery stable. The exact cause has never been determined. Although both the Whitehall and Montague fire departments responded promptly, the blaze took all the wooden buildings on both sides of Colby Street, a block of brick buildings on the north, and Baker's brick drugstore on the south.

Greetings from Muskegon, Mich.
Western Ave., Looking West.

Opposite page, top, left: *Not even the county courthouse escaped the Pine Street Fire of 1891. Volunteers removed some of the contents but then could only stand by helplessly as the fire spread to the structure's roof. Courtesy, The Muskegon Collection, Hackley Public Library*

Opposite page, top, right: *The old Cummings House on Pine Street was another of the buildings destroyed in the Pine Street Fire. A total of 250 businesses and homes were destroyed before it was checked. Courtesy, Charles H. Yates Collection, Muskegon County Museum*

Opposite page, bottom, left: *Whitehall, like all lumber towns, was always in danger of fire. A major fire hit the White Lake community on September 19, 1890, just nine years after its first inferno. Courtesy, Muskegon Chronicle*

Opposite page, bottom, right: *This 1906 view of Western Avenue, looking east from Third Street, illustrates how quickly Muskegon recovered after the Pine Street Fire. Courtesy, Charles H. Yates Collection, Muskegon County Museum*

The flames leapt rapidly from one wooden building to another and with the aid of a southwest gale easily crossed the street. It was soon apparent that the entire business district would go and efforts were made to keep any mills from being destroyed.

The booming company's tug, *Peter Dalton,* came as close to shore as possible and threw a stream of water from its hose. A Muskegon steam fire engine was called for by telegraph and it was loaded on a train. But the order was countermanded as the fire came under control. This was just as well since the wooden railroad tunnel under Colby Street burned and it was several days before the debris could be cleared from the track to permit a train to come through from Muskegon.

Virtually every able-bodied adult in Whitehall and Montague turned out to fight the fire but the flames defied all efforts. After destroying the buildings on Colby Street, the fire attacked buildings on Mears Avenue. It stopped just a few feet short of the Mears Hotel (later the Whitehall Hotel which, ironically, burned in May 1938). The hotel was saved by quick work by a group of mill hands who removed a burning shed and the adjoining burning wood sidewalk. The fire jumped to the next block and swept to the swamp, destroying more houses and buildings before it burned out.

What happened to Whitehall was comparable to the Chicago fire of 1871 and the Muskegon fire of 1874. The busy community was in ashes with losses estimated at about $150,000 and insurance to cover only about $54,000. There is no record of human life lost in the blaze but eleven fine horses from Sturtevant's livery perished.

Also like Muskegon, Whitehall rapidly rebuilt and moved farther to the north and west. An area of about five acres in the heart of the city was destroyed and the business district was later built up away from Lake Street and beyond the old railroad tunnel. But on September 19, 1890, a second fire hit. This one started in an icehouse on the dock along the hill side of town. Thirty-two buildings and a number of houses burned with losses set at about $50,000.

Once again the town rebuilt and soon after, the fire threat to the county diminished with the demise of the lumbering industry.

*   *   *

In this era of reconstruction after the fires came the Spanish-American War and, again, Muskegon was quick to volunteer. In 1884 Company G, First Michigan Infantry, was organized with Captain John R. Bennett in command. Among the recruits were

several marksmen, veterans of the Civil War. Called the Muskegon Rifles, it was considered the best drilled and best shooting outfit in the state.

The Michigan National Guard was formed March 28, 1891, and the Rifles became Company C of the Thirty-fourth Michigan regiment. War with Spain broke out in April 1898 and the Rifles were mustered into service. The company trained in Michigan and Virginia and was later sent to Cuba, where it was in reserve at San Juan Hill to support Teddy Roosevelt's "Rough Riders." The Rifles also served at Santiago and San Diego. There were no battle casualties but the Rifles lost nine men to malaria.

When they returned home it was to a dying city. The revitalizing bond program was still in its early stages. There was a huge welcome but little work for the veterans in the worn-out lumber industry.

The turn of the century brought new industries, however, and they were a varied lot. They ranged from a curled hair mattress company, to piano companies and furniture companies, to a maker of chemical fire extinguishers, even to an automobile company, the Henry Motor Car Company. None of these industries survive today, but they did their part in pulling Muskegon through a most difficult economic period.

*   *   *

Just before World War I, two summer-related features brought fame to Muskegon. One was the Actors Colony and Theatrical Colony Yacht Club, the other—vast publicity in Chicago papers, calling the county's resorts "The Riviera of the West."

Theatrical people began settling in Muskegon in significant numbers about 1911. Most of them were vaudevillians, many

Above: *Sergeant R.E. Ashley of the Muskegon Rifles is shown in his dress uniform before departure to the war in Cuba in 1898. Courtesy, Charles H. Yates Collection, Muskegon County Museum*

Above, left: *The Muskegon Rifles posed for this 1898 photograph, with their lamb and dog mascots, prior to their shipment to Cuba during the Spanish-American War. Courtesy, Charles H. Yates Collection, Muskegon County Museum*

Opposite page, top: *Members of Local Union No. 100 of the United Brotherhood of Carpenters and Joiners are decked out in their finery for the Labor Day Parade in 1899. Courtesy, Charles H. Yates Collection, Muskegon County Museum*

Opposite page, bottom: *One of the hazards of parades in downtown Muskegon around the turn of the century was that they were liable to be disrupted by streetcars. Here a streetcar splits the line of march during the Labor Day Parade in 1892 at the junction of Western and Market. Courtesy, Charles H. Yates Collection, Muskegon County Museum*

had played the Lake Michigan Theater. Of all the places they travelled through in their forty weeks of work, Muskegon seemed the ideal place to have summer homes. The first to settle in Bluffton in 1905 were Joe Keaton, William "Mush" Rawls, and Lew Earl.

In 1909 C.S. "Pop" Ford acquired cut-over Bluffton timberland from David Irwin, a pioneer businessman. The land was platted and 200 lots were sold to actors.

Keaton, his wife Myra, and son Buster were probably the best known of the group. Buster was just a small boy when the family first came to the area. He was thrown about the stage with wreckless abandon by his father as the feature of their act. Later he became one of the best known silent screen comedians. He always reminisced about his summers in Muskegon with great affection and was a life member of the Muskegon Elks Lodge.

Other famous residents included Mr. and Mrs. Max Gruber who had an animal act with a zebra, dog, and an elephant named Little Eva. The act toured the country and Europe with great success. Gruber died in Muskegon in 1939.

Eventually the actors' community disbanded, but the Theatrical Colony Yacht Club, which was very active while the actors colony was going strong, has survived. It is now called the Muskegon Yacht Club.

The same summer features which attracted the actors—cool lake breezes, an ideal climate, and a quiet change from hot, noisy cities—began to bring many visitors from midwestern cities like Chicago, Cincinnati, Detroit, and Cleveland, coming by way of the Goodrich Steamship Line and by railroad.

A number of resorts sprang up from the White Lake area in the north to the Mona Lake area in the south. Resort development in the White Lake area, albeit very informal, began about

Above: *A popular Muskegon face is that of veteran character actor Harry Morgan. A graduate of Muskegon High School as Harry Bratsburg, he's appeared as Colonel Sherman Potter in the television show "M*A*S*H*." Courtesy,* Muskegon Chronicle

Top, right: *The Theatrical Colony Yacht Club was an adjunct of the Actors' Colony in Bluffton just before World War I. It is now the Muskegon Yacht Club. This 1912 photograph shows a crowd at one of the many regattas staged by the club. Courtesy, The Muskegon Collection, Hackley Public Library*

Right: *Max Gruber is shown with his elephant, Little Eva, his zebra, and dog in this circa 1930 photograph. Gruber was the last remnant of the old Actor's Colony in Bluffton. He died in 1939. Courtesy, Charles H. Yates Collection, Muskegon County Museum*

1870 and boomed in the mid-1890s with the establishment of Michillinda in 1894 and Sylvan Beach a year later. Both were located on the south side of White Lake near its mouth. By World War I White Lake had twenty-seven resorts with five more just to the south along Lake Michigan, three others on Duck Lake and two more on Blue Lake, adjacent to the White River.

Around Mona Lake were the Lake Harbor Hotel, which could accommodate 500 people, and the Bellevue, and Antisdales hotels. At Muskegon Heights were the Ancel, Heights, and Taylor hotels. At Lake Michigan Park were the Lake Michigan Park Hotel and McGowans. North Muskegon had the Lakeview House and the Rienzi, and the Pen Bryn and Westmeath were on the shores of Bear Lake. Lakewood had the Lakeview Clubhouse. It was, indeed, the "Riviera of the West."

1919 STREETCAR RIOT
CAUSED BY PENNY INCREASE

A group of Muskegon youngsters mugged for the camera around an overturned streetcar the morning after the streetcar riot. Courtesy, Muskegon Chronicle

Muskegon County is generally known as a relatively quiet place. Such was not the case on the night of August 6, 1919. The city of Muskegon erupted into a raging mob that included thousands and almost thoroughly destroyed the rolling stock and property of the Muskegon Traction and Lighting Company, which owned the streetcars.

What brought it all about was an increase in streetcar fare from six cents to seven cents which took effect August 1. Despite considerable grumbling on the part of residents, the fare increase on a Friday was not met with any outward disturbance.

A statement by Mayor John H. Moore and City Attorney William Carpenter called for patience from the city residents pending a satisfactory solution at a city commission meeting called for August 5. The meeting turned out to be a disaster. A proposed ten-year franchise and an ordinance to regulate the fare were killed because of the absence of one alderman.

The meeting room was jammed with irate factory workers, the primary streetcar riders and the ones to bear the fare increase. Reports told of a rowdy crowd that was shouting considerably. A large dog somehow got into the chamber and added its loud barks to the confusion, according to newspaper accounts.

The riot started about six o'clock the next night. A group of workers tried to ride for six cents on a car at the Jefferson Avenue switch. When informed by the conductor that the fare was now seven cents, they refused to pay and pushed the car to a siding.

Other cars began to jam up at the intersection and a large crowd gathered. By 7:30 p.m. a crowd of men began to push cars off the tracks. The police arrived but the crowd was too large to be controlled. By 8:00 p.m. the crowd, which had now become an angry mob, began pushing streetcars into one another.

By 10:00 p.m. the mob became violent and began to destroy the cars and any company property it could find. One group, estimated by witnesses to number about 1,000, marched to the carbarns at Franklin and Michigan. This group demolished the barns and the cars in them as a crowd of several thousand cheered them on.

Rioting spread throughout the city. Cars were stopped and tipped over. Everything possible was ripped from the cars, windows were broken, seats were torn out and burned. Police began firing warning shots into the air in an attempt to stop the mobs, but the badly outnumbered officers were forced to flee for their lives.

Rioters began to push the cars down the hill at Pine and Jefferson. Thirteen cars were demolished as they smashed into one another. Three others were left smashed along Jefferson. When the sun came up the next morning, downtown Muskegon was a scene of massive destruction. Wrecked streetcars and company property was strewn everywhere.

The *Muskegon Chronicle*'s extra of that night carried a front-page editorial entitled, "Muskegon's Disgrace." It read in part:

Muskegon stands today before its neighboring municipalities of the state and nation a city disgraced. We have been advertised to the utmost borders of the nation as a city of hoodlums and thugs.

People were urged to stay off the streets the next day, and an investigation was launched. Eleven riot suspects were arraigned in court August 11. Some eventually went to prison. One person died of injuries sustained in the riot. Mayor Moore announced that the fare would remain at six cents and he would use police power to enforce it, so the Muskegon Traction and Lighting Company would not be allowed to raise the price again.

Rolling stock was repaired and replaced and streetcars began running again. The company suddenly became public-relations conscious and began explaining to the public the problems of increased competition from buses and automobiles and increased labor costs. The public seemed to understand because it always favored streetcars over buses in referendums.

In the early 1920s the automobile increasingly became the main mode of transportation and the streetcar was doomed. The total of 4,328,752 revenue passengers carried here in 1920 dropped to almost half that number in 1928. Streetcars once carried the bulk of blue-collar workers but in eight years the number dropped to only a fraction of the labor force as the automobile and buses took over.

Service ended October 19, 1929, and company property was sold or scrapped. Most of the rails were torn up or merely paved over. According to veteran director of public works and utilities, Louis VanDinther, the last remaining streetcar tracks—at Thompson and Edgewater—were covered with blacktop more than twenty-five years ago.

Muskegon Mayor John H. Moore (left) and Muskegon Heights Mayor Martin Schoenberg engaged in a spike-driving contest when the Muskegon Railway and Navigation Company short-line railroad (commonly called the Belt Line) was built in 1919. It provided rail facilities around the extensive manufacturing districts in each city. Moore missed striking his spike; Schoenberg hit his and was declared the winner. Courtesy, Charles H. Yates Collection, Muskegon County Museum

5 *The Arsenal of Democracy*

When World War I came along, Muskegon was once again ready to fight. The Muskegon Rifles had remained in the National Guard as Company I of the Second Michigan. It was called into federal service in 1916 when Pancho Villa caused an incident on the Mexican border. Under Captain Carl Field some 150 men were sent to Waco, Texas where they were on patrol duty for several months, although not engaged in any skirmishes.

The United States' neutrality in the world war ended April 6, 1917, when war was declared against Germany. The first draft called 178 Muskegon County men into service September 19, 1917, but already many volunteers had gone over. The Rifles were on the firing line at Alsace in France by June 18. Many county men were part of the Thirty-second (Red Arrow) Division and they fought at the Meuse, Argonne, in the campaigns of the Aisne-Oise, and Aisne-Marne. Some local men even served from 1918-1919 in Archangel, Russia, as members of the "Polar Bears," so named because of the severe arctic winter they experienced.

Some 3,000 Muskegon County men and women saw service and of those, 104 gave their lives. Among those killed in action was Captain Merritt Lamb, the father of the Muskegon Boy Scouts. Some received major decorations from the United States and foreign governments. These included Sergeant Lyman T. Covell—later the county sheriff—and Amy Beers, a member of the United States Nurse Corps and later superintendent of nurses at Hackley Hospital.

*   *   *

By the time of the "Roaring '20s," Muskegon County was largely optimistic. After all, the "War to End All Wars" had just ended with the victorious allies prevailing over the hated Huns.

In addition, Muskegon had survived the economic devastation of the lumber boom collapse, a number of varied industries had opened their doors, and the area had established itself as a tourist mecca. The general outlook could be classified as "promising."

Prior to 1925 the various bonus funds had brought to the city forty-two new industries, seventeen of which were still operating in the late 1950s. Some steel industries were started but failed because of the distance from supplies and markets. Muskegon had better luck with automobile-related industries.

When Continental Motors Corporation manufactured an engine in the early 1920s which powered an early Indianapolis 500 winner, there was a great demand for its engines. To meet the demand the company needed castings. At this time three Chicago men, Don Campbell, Ira Wyant, and George W. Cannon, had a small foundry in Chicago but needed more space. They saw an advertisement offering space and also a large supply of pig iron in the Racine Boat Works. The three came to Muskegon and with their last $157 made the model required by Continental. In time, Campbell, Wyant and Cannon became the largest gray iron foundry in the world. It now exists as the CWC Castings Division of Textron, Inc. Unfortunately the main plant will move to Indiana in 1986, costing 450 jobs. However, the divi-

Below: Muskegon sent its sons to war by way of the Chesapeake and Ohio Railroad depot on Western Avenue. This photo was taken in 1913. Courtesy, Charles H. Yates Collection, Muskegon County Museum

Opposite page, top: Captain Merritt Lamb, the father of the Boy Scouts in Muskegon, was among those killed in action in World War I. A local American Legion post is named after him. Courtesy, Muskegon Chronicle

Opposite page, bottom: Muskegon has had a farmers market since 1921, shown here. It was first called the City Market and was located between Clay at Ottawa, and Eastern at Cedar. Courtesy, Charles H. Yates Collection, Muskegon County Museum

sion headquarters will be staying in Muskegon and another plant will be slightly expanded.

Other success stories soon followed. Sealed Power Corporation and Muskegon Piston Ring Company became major world suppliers of automobile engine accessories. Several pattern plants developed in the area, also dependent on the automobile industry.

*   *   *

With times generally good, Muskegonites began to spend more attention to recreation and sports. The area had been noted from the time of the early explorers as a hunting and fishing haven. Deer, rabbit, squirrel, waterfowl, and other game birds, though once abounding in great numbers, are still present. The early settlers killed the now-extinct passenger pigeon by the millions as the birds congregated around Pigeon Hill. Game fish such as lake, rainbow, brown, brook trout, walleye, and northern pike were plentiful in Lake Michigan and inland waters. Panfish, of which perch always has been the king, could be caught by the bucketful.

As far as sports were concerned, high school football was the

Right: *Pigeon Hill, shown in this 1928 photograph, no longer exists due to sand mining but the site has since become Harbour Town, a complex of marinas, commercial businesses, and condominiums. Courtesy,* Muskegon Chronicle

Opposite page, top: *The Muskegon Fire Department displayed this combination chemical and hose truck decked out with flags for a 1924 parade. Courtesy, Charles H. Yates Collection, Muskegon County Museum*

Opposite page, bottom: *After several starts, dating back to the first one in 1871, funds finally were raised to build a YMCA in the winter of 1925-26. Here a crowd watches a worker post the progress of the fund drive on a clock in Federal Square. The building was dedicated from November 26 to December 3, 1927. It later became the YFCA and has since been converted to luxury apartments at the site of Second and Clay. Courtesy, Charles H. Yates Collection, Muskegon County Museum*

big organized sport. The Muskegon High School Big Reds, who began competing in 1895, was the only school to represent the area until 1920 when Muskegon Heights High School began as a Class D school. Muskegon's rise to prominence began in 1906 when Robert C. Zuppke began his coaching career. He went on to become a legendary coach at the University of Illinois and subsequently was voted into the football Hall of Fame. Zuppke introduced two football innovations in his two-year stay in Muskegon. First, he insisted that his teams be uniformed. This meant dying sweatshirts and stockings in the school colors. Each player had to buy his own pants and shoes and his mother had to sew quilted protection into the uniform.

Zuppke's second innovation was the spiral snap from center. In the days before the T-formation, this was a most important manuever, giving Muskegon teams a big advantage until it became universal. A local man, Lester Nelson, actually invented this pass but Zuppke immediately saw its potential and developed it.

Muskegon High School became a football powerhouse in the state under coaches Louis Gudelsky, J. Francis Jacks, and C. Leo Redmond. Redmond's teams ran up unbeaten strings of thirty-seven, twenty-eight, and fifteen games during his tenure. One of the other stars in the early 1920s was Bennie Oosterbaan who later gained All-American honors at the University of Michigan and coached the Wolverines.

Before the turn of the century, Muskegon teams played at Castenholz Park and later at Driving Park at Lakeside. Charles Hackley donated the ground now known as Hackley Stadium in 1906 and the games were moved there. It wasn't until 1914 that solid wooden bleachers which seated 3,000 were erected at the field at a cost of $2,400. Later temporary bleachers were placed at the other side of the field and behind the end zones to increase the capacity to 6,500. In 1920 a fundraising project was started for a permanent grandstand; it was built in 1927 at a cost of $68,000. The concrete stand seated 6,283 and with new bleachers surrounding the rest of the field, the capacity was raised to more than 12,000.

Muskegon Heights also gained state prominence in football in the mid 1930s when its Tigers went thirty-two games without a defeat. Another long string of twenty-seven straight victories took place in the mid-1940s. Coach Oscar E. "Okie" Johnson guided the Tigers for more than thirty years. Home games were played in Phillips Field which was built in 1925 and seated close to 10,000. Everett "Sonny" Grandelius went on to gain All-American honors at Michigan State University. He later played professional football for the New York Giants and coached at Colorado University.

Baseball was the oldest of organized sports in Muskegon with the Tryus nine playing in 1869 at "Mason's Forty." A professional team was formed in 1883 and entered the old Northwestern League with Grand Rapids and Bay City; Fort Wayne, Indiana; Peoria, Illinois; Milwaukee, Wisconsin; and St. Paul and Minneapolis, Minnesota. The first grandstand was on Strong Avenue; later an enclosed field was built where the Redmond-Potter gym now stands at the former site of Mercy Hospital. Because of the distance between cities, the league folded after several years. The Muskegon team then played in a league made up of Michigan cities—Grand Rapids, Lansing, Saginaw, Flint, and Battle Creek. The site of games was switched to the Driving Park when it was built in the Lakeside area in the 1880s.

One of the top baseball players in those days was Archie DeBaker who has since become known as the "grand old man"

Opposite page, top: *Charles H. Hackley donated the land for Muskegon High School's athletic field in 1906. This photograph shows Hackley Stadium just after wooden stands had been erected. A permanent cement stadium was erected in 1927 and the capacity increased to about 12,000. Courtesy, Charles H. Yates Collection, Muskegon County Museum*

Opposite page, bottom: *Fishing for perch off the old south pier was a popular pastime in the early 1900s. The barges in the background are working on what is now the south breakwater and lighthouse. This photograph was taken in 1928. Courtesy, Charles H. Yates Collection, Muskegon County Museum*

of local baseball. He played the game for more than twenty years and then managed the Muskegon Reds. The Muskegon teams played in a succession of state leagues which were organized with great hopes but which folded after a few years.

Modern baseball really arrived just before World War I when native Charles W. Marsh headed the Central League with teams from Indiana, Illinois, and Michigan. Marsh also donated land at the corner of Peck and Laketon for a field, which still bears his name. The field was enclosed and a grandstand erected; it became one of the best minor league parks for its size in the nation. Marsh Field is still used by local amateur teams; all that remains of the field's old wooden stands is the concrete base.

Still, the "try-but-fold" league system continued until 1952 when the death knell sounded for minor leagues, and professional baseball ended in the area. The Detroit Tigers backed a team here in 1940 but the league folded when World War II started. The Chicago White Sox and later the New York Yankees had Muskegon teams called the Clippers in the old Central League, both of which bowed out in 1952.

Over the years, players who went on to become big names in the major leagues performed in Muskegon. Among the best known was "Fat" Freddie Fitzsimmons, who was one of the top pitchers in baseball for twenty-one years, most of them with the New

Minor league baseball enjoyed some success in the Muskegon area in the late 1940s and early 1950s. This photo of Marsh Field, a donation from Charles Marsh, shows the old grandstand and bleachers in about 1950. The field became one of the best minor league parks for its size in the nation. Courtesy, The Muskegon Collection, Hackley Public Library

These Muskegon Lassies drew 147,000 fans to Marsh Field during the All-American Girls Professional Baseball League season in 1947. Five years later the league folded. Courtesy, The Muskegon Collection, Hackley Public Library

York Giants. Then there were Elston Howard, a star catcher for years with the New York Yankees; Jim Greengrass, who toiled for the Cincinnati Reds; and Stubby Overmire, John Lipon, and John McHale who played with the Detroit Tigers.

Muskegon women had a brief field day when the city hosted a team in the All-American Girls Professional Baseball League. The league flourished from 1946 into the early 1950s. The local team, the Lassies, played at Marsh Field when the Clippers were on the road. The Lassies attracted 147,000 fans in 1947 playing against teams from Battle Creek, Kalamazoo, and Grand Rapids; South Bend and Fort Wayne, Indiana; Kenosha, Wisconsin; and Peoria and Rockford, Illinois.

Sports such as golf, tennis, sailing, and bowling have also flourished in the county since the 1920s. With much bowling equipment being manufactured locally by Brunswick, it is not surprising that Ernest Hedenskoog from Muskegon invented and perfected the automatic pinsetter—now an integral part of every bowling alley in the world.

*　　*　　*

In 1927 Muskegon enjoyed an oil boom which looked like it might replace the vanished lumber boom as an economic answer

Above: *The causeway between Muskegon and North Muskegon as it looked before landscaping. This aerial photograph was taken in the early 1930s. The B.C. Cobb plant, a coal-burning electric power plant, appears at the upper right before its large smokestack was erected. Courtesy,* Muskegon Chronicle

Opposite page: *This Muskegon Township oil gusher came in on December 17, 1927, and sparked a brief but frenzied oil boom; the end came about two years later when Standard Oil Company dropped the price of crude from $1.26 to fifty cents a barrel. Courtesy, The Muskegon Collection, Hackley Public Library*

to all its problems. Back in the 1880s mill owners sought salt deposits, hoping to use their facilities and mill wastes to convert brine to salt. They drilled but failed to reach the saline deposits and became discouraged when they found traces of oil. There were no automobiles in those days and there was little demand for oil except for refining it into kerosene for lamps. Although oil drilling didn't seem to them to be worth their efforts, the mill owners did keep logs; these reports later became the basis for the region's oil development.

Stanley Daniloff, a former tailor, pioneered the Muskegon field. He organized and was president of the Muskegon Oil Corporation. Daniloff raised $79,000 for the drilling operations. In 1927 the first well was drilled east of the city on the old Grand Rapids Road. The next well was drilled in Muskegon Township on the Charles Reeths farm. Oil burst out with a gush on December 17, 1927. There was at first little confidence in Daniloff's venture by the general public but skepticism washed away in the rush of gushing oil.

Suddenly Muskegon was in the midst of another boom. A strange group of people arrived to an area which had resumed its calm demeanor after the 1919 streetcar riot. There were lease-hounds, capitalists, drillers, machinists, and oil field laborers. In 1927 leases for tracts of ninety acres which had been obtained for one dollar per tract shot up to $2,500 an acre just within a few months. Most leases after the first flurry averaged out at $500 an acre. Muskegon suddenly became the largest oil producing field in Michigan. Drillers were making ten dollars a day and machinists were getting nine dollars—incredible wages for the time.

A total of 1,928 barrels were produced that first December. In 1928 the total reached 334,601 and by the next year it had increased ten times to 3,157,668 barrels. By then more than 450 wells had been drilled and there was a proven field of 2,800 acres.

But the boom ended almost as soon as it began. Standard Oil Company announced on February 7, 1929, that it had dropped the price of Dundee crude oil from $1.26 to fifty cents a barrel. With a price of fifty cents a barrel everything stopped in the Muskegon fields. Some drillers just left everything the way it was and departed. Others drilled to just above the Dundee and capped their wells. The 1,000 men employed in the oil fields at high wages suddenly were out of work and most of them left for better fields.

Not everything was lost, however. The Muskegon Chamber of Commerce, feeling that there might be an end to the supply of

oil, sought capital which would invest in refineries so the product could be refined locally. And so Muskegon became a large gasoline storage operation. Gulf and Socony Vacuum established tank farms, an Old Dutch refinery was established, and in 1931 Walter E. Anderson began the Naph-Sol Refining Company (now Zephyr, Inc.), which grew into the largest independent distributor of petroleum products in the state, and one of the largest in the nation.

*   *   *

With the advent of the automobile and the bus came the demise of the streetcar. The last trolley ran on October 19, 1929 and with it, the last of the tracks and wires. Although referendums over a period of more than thirty years had purported the streetcar to be unbeatable in public transportation, the system was rigidly locked to its tracks. Even after the Streetcar Riot of 1919 the public supported streetcars to the extent that the city council at one time barred competitive bus lines. But the system was doomed. After carrying a total of 4,328,752 passengers in 1920, the figure dropped to 2,769,817 in 1928.

Close on the heels of the oil business and trolley system decline came the Great Depression. Muskegon, like every other region in the nation, suffered. The local economy was not hit severely until late in 1931 when two banks went under—Peoples Bank and the First State Bank of Muskegon Heights. Three others managed to survive—Hackley Bank, Muskegon Savings Bank, and Lumberman's Bank. They came out intact after the state and national bank holidays of 1933. In the state 75 percent of the

Opposite page, far left: *The Flatiron Building, which occupied a triangular plot of ground opposite Federal Square, was a landmark in Muskegon from 1912 until it was razed to make way for the Muskegon Mall in 1976. This photo was taken circa 1930. Courtesy, Charles H. Yates Collection, Muskegon County Museum*

Opposite page, left: *In 1927 one of Muskegon's busiest corners was the intersection of First and Western, later site of the Muskegon Mall. The Hackley Union National Bank is on the left, which in two years would become the Hackley and Union National Bank. Courtesy, Charles H. Yates Collection, Muskegon County Museum*

Opposite page, bottom: *This is how Western Avenue looked in 1928 looking west on Western Avenue from the Lyman Block. Courtesy, Charles H. Yates Collection, Muskegon County Museum*

Right: *Muskegon's first airmail service began July 17, 1928, from the Continental Airport. Postmaster Lincoln Rodgers (left) supervised the loading of the Thompson Aeronautical Company plane. Courtesy, Charles H. Yates Collection, Muskegon County Museum*

banks went out of business. It turned out that the economic conservatism bred by the panics of 1903 and 1907 and the wild business cycles helped Muskegon survive.

The number of wage earners in Muskegon County dropped from 18,087 in July 1929 to 12,632 just six months later. The figure fell to 6,314 in December 1932. Most factories were open only two or three days a week as orders dropped off. The city welfare load became so heavy that Muskegon instituted a "man-a-block" program in which each block was responsible for employing one man a week to perform various odd jobs. Residents chipped in fifty cents a day among them to pay for his services. With the aid of churches, the Salvation Army, Red Cross, Welfare Mission, and other organizations, no one went hungry.

Muskegon industrialists introduced a "share-the-work" movement which attracted national attention. This idea was the brainchild of L.C. Walker of the Shaw-Walker Company and drew support from some forty local plants. But the problem with this plan was that each laborer worked only half the number of hours for half the wages. It drew criticism from labor leaders and economists because even though it took men off welfare and gave them a part-time job, it did not improve their lot significantly.

There was still some brightness in this bleak era. In 1937 the city celebrated its centennial with a mammoth stockade on the Mart and Grand Trunk properties. The celebration lasted for fifteen days and included a number of exhibits depicting Muskegon's history, particularly the lumbering era.

The Depression ended in Muskegon with the advent of the 1940s when defense orders began to pile up. Continental Motors Manufacturing Company, for instance, went from 700 workers to

nearly 5,000 with orders to produce tank and airplane engines. The plant rapidly expanded to include the company's old holdings on the hill at Getty Street which had been the site of the Continental Airport.

Other booming defense industries during the 1940s included foundries like Campbell, Wyant and Cannon and the Lakey Foundry, both of which employed thousands. A severe labor shortage required recruiters to turn to the south; a number of blacks arrived to keep the furnaces going. Many have remained to become a part of the county's population. Brunswick, at one time a manufacturer of everything from automobile tires, phonographs, radios and records, to bowling and billiards equipment, was also heavily involved in war production. Today the Muskegon firm manufactures only bowling and billiards products.

The National Guard contingent in Muskegon had remained active after World War I and, although no one thought Americans would ever have to fight again, Company G left for Louisiana October 25, 1940, as 20,000 bid them farewell. Only a month later the first contingent of draftees left for military service. The first local casualty was Homer David Hopkins, who was aboard the U.S.S. *Arizona* when the Japanese struck Pearl Harbor on December 7, 1941. The next day war was declared; immediately enlistments swelled and draft calls were stepped up. Muskegon County men and women served all over the world and there was hardly a major battle or small skirmish that did not include someone from the county.

Opposite page, far left: *Muskegon celebrated its centennial in July of 1937 with a carnival. This mammoth stockade enclosed buildings and surrounding businesses with exhibits on the Mart and Grand Trunk properties. Courtesy, Charles H. Yates Collection, Muskegon County Museum*

Opposite page, left: *As part of the Muskegon Centennial in 1937, this log drive down the Muskegon River was staged. It was a stark contrast to the river of logs of the 1880s. Courtesy,* Muskegon Chronicle

Right: *Brunswick-Balke-Collender, as shown in this aerial view in 1936, was one of the first firms brought to Muskegon by the early bonus plans. It now survives as Brunswick Corporation and has its corporate headquarters in Muskegon. Courtesy, Charles H. Yates Collection, Muskegon County Museum*

With the surrender of Japan on August 14, 1945, men and women returned home. There was no civic celebration because they came home singly from different parts of the world. The big celebrations occurred within each family circle. The cost to Muskegon County in lives was 318 with fifteen missing.

By the end of World War II some 36,000 persons worked in area industries. The pre-war average was 14,000.

But hard times hit again in 1948 when the post-war demand for automobiles and appliances subsided. Muskegon essentially was a parts supplier with more than half the industries involved in automobile production. The city had no control over the finished product and many automobile manufacturers were developing their own parts plants. Returning veterans again faced a dismal job market.

*   *   *

On top of the job shortage, shortly after the war on the night of Friday, February 22, 1946 Muskegon City suffered its greatest fire damage. While this so-called "Hardy Fire" didn't cover the extent of the two previous big fires in 1874 and 1891, it caused damage estimated at two million dollars as buildings on the south side of Western Avenue between First and Second streets were wiped out. Nearly every fireman in the county had a hand in battling the blaze or standing by in the event of other emergencies.

The fire had started in the paper storage section in the William D. Hardy Company store's basement. The cause was never determined but an automatic alarm was turned in at 9:00 p.m. Before the fire was brought under control at 1:30 a.m. Saturday, the following businesses and city sections were destroyed: the Hardy store; the Hubbard block housing the Neumode Hosiery Company, Daniels Company, and the Paul J. Schlossman offices; the Dearborn block housing Mangel's Women's Wear; the Krautheim block; the Montgomery block housing Buel's shoe store and Walgreen's Drugs; and numerous second-story professional offices.

Word spread throughout the city and at the height of the fire an estimated crowd of 25,000 people gathered to watch. High wind and cold weather added to the dangers. The temperature was twenty-eight degrees and several inches of water covered the street. Burning embers blew at least two blocks. The fire's westward spread was stopped by a fire wall on the west side of the old Montgomery Ward building at the corner of Second Street; this building was not destroyed but so damaged by smoke and water that it had to be rebuilt.

Over just a twenty year span, the county had thus survived everything from two world wars and the Great Depression to the great Hardy fire, while it enjoyed a brief oil boom and many athletic triumphs.

Above and right: *The Hardy's Fire of February 22, 1946, caused about two million dollars worth of damage—Muskegon's most expensive fire to date. An estimated 25,000 spectators viewed the fire that night and the next morning.* Courtesy, Muskegon Chronicle

THE U.S.S. *MUSKEGON* NEVER VISITED ITS NAMESAKE

Like many municipalities, Muskegon had a ship named for it during World War II but oddly enough, the ship never visited Muskegon nor did anyone from the city or the county ever serve on her.

To the men who served on the U.S.S. *Muskegon,* she was known as the "Mighty Musk." To the United States Navy and Coast Guard she was known as Patrol Frigate 24. This only war vessel named after the city was built in Superior, Wisconsin, at the Walter Butler Shipyards Inc., and launched July 25, 1943. She was towed down the Mississippi River to New Orleans where she was commissioned in February 1944 for active service as a convoy escort during the final years of the war.

Secretary of the Navy Frank Knox suggested in a letter to then-Muskegon Mayor Gustov L. Lundborg that a sponsor be selected for the vessel, someone to break the traditional bottle over the bow and christen it before it took to the water. Mrs. Alma Hopkins was named by the Muskegon City Commission as the sponsor of the ship. She was the mother of Seaman First Class Homer David Hopkins, the first local Navy man to lose his life in World War II, dying in the flaming hull of the battleship U.S.S. *Arizona* at Pearl Harbor on December 7, 1941.

The *Muskegon* cost $1.7 million to build and was similar in design to the famed Canadian corvettes that made names for themselves as watchdogs of the North Atlantic convoys to Great Britain and Russia. The ship was 310 feet long, had a speed of thirty-seven knots, and was propelled by steam turbines developing 5,500 horsepower. She weighed 1,500 tons and carried a crew of 130, along with five-inch guns, anti-aircraft guns, and depth charges.

The crew members came from all over the country, but none from Muskegon. Records show that a dozen or so were trained at the Grand Haven Coast Guard Training Center.

The Muskegon City Commission adopted a resolution asking the Secretary of the Navy to allow the ship to make a stopover in Muskegon on its trip from Lake Superior to the Gulf of Mexico. Yet this was not to be. Rear Admiral E.S. Land, chairman of the maritime commission under whose direction the vessel was built and who retained control of its movements until it was delivered to the navy at New Orleans, said the ship could not stop in Muskegon.

Land's reason was, "[a] very close schedule program will not permit delaying delivery of the *Muskegon* in order that it might stop over at the city for which it is named."

A photostatic copy of the *Muskegon*'s war history was presented to James L. Gillard, Muskegon's mayor in 1946, at a Navy Day dinner at the Occidental Hotel. The records show that during World War II the ship was under U.S. Navy command but crewed by Coast Guardsmen. It served two years in the Atlantic Ocean on submarine patrol and weather research duty.

After sea trials, the *Muskegon* was ordered to the Pacific, but shortly after clearing the Panama Canal was ordered to return to Boston for duty. Arriving in Boston early in October 1944, the ship underwent conversion as a weather ship and in the first week of November headed to the Naval Operating Base in Argentia, Newfoundland, for duty.

After some service in the Bermuda area, the *Muskegon* took over what the war record called a "highly dan-

The frigate U.S.S. *Muskegon carried the city's name on convoy duty during World War II. She was scrapped in the late 1960s. Courtesy, Muskegon Chronicle*

gerous mission" early in 1945—carrying 1,000 hedgehogs (depth bombs) from Boston to Argentia. According to the records "every available compartment, the deck space and even the passages were filled with ammunition." The ship sailed at full speed to its destination without incident.

After the war the *Muskegon* and twenty-eight other frigates were converted to serve the Coast Guard as rescue ships and weather stations in the Atlantic. Particular duties involved monitoring trans-Atlantic commercial aircraft such as the old Pan-American Clippers. The Coast Guard kept pilots informed of weather and the ships were available for rescue, if needed.

The *Muskegon* was back in New Orleans serving as a Coast Guard cutter in 1946. In August of that year she was decommissioned by the Coast Guard and returned to the U.S. Navy.

What became of the "Mighty Musk?" She changed her colors, country, and name. According to the records, the navy sold the *Muskegon* to France on March 26, 1947. The frigate was commissioned in the French navy on the same day. Under the French Ministry of Transport and Public Works she was renamed the *Mermoz F-14.* Stripped of her armament, she served as a weather ship off the French coast until she was scrapped in the late 1950s.

Urry Arch, standing in front of Muskegon City Hall, is a familiar landmark to residents throughout the county. Famed New York artist Steven Urry sculpted the arch out of aluminum. It stood in Grand Rapids for two years until Dr. Robert Swendenburg purchased it for the city in 1975, as a memorial to his wife. Photo by David Carlson. Courtesy, David Carlson

6 *Muskegon on the Move*

War again appeared on the horizon as Muskegon headed into the second half of the twentieth century. Once more Muskegon County sent its young men and women into action in the Korean conflict and fifty-five of them failed to return alive. Once more Muskegon's foundries and other industries were geared for the war effort.

The end of hostilities in 1953 caused a lull in the local economy. But in 1958 a singular event, the opening of the St. Lawrence Seaway, brought what many hoped would be once and for all economic stability for the county.

Ever since the boom days of Muskegon's lumber industry, the city was recognized as having the finest port on the east side of Lake Michigan and certainly one of the finest on the entire Great Lakes. Muskegon City had carried for years, and still does, the appellation of "Port City." There was a shipping lull after the lumber boom but it was revived in the 1920s and 1930s with the construction of a modern arrowhead breakwater at the harbor entrance, the beginning of the car ferry service between Muskegon and Milwaukee, and the erection of the Mart—a port terminal built at a cost of 1.2 million dollars by the West Michigan Dock and Market Corporation.

The port was thus equipped to handle overseas vessels and the first one, the *S.S. Glitrefjell* of the Norwegian Fjell Line, arrived in Muskegon May 8, 1935. Muskegon found itself in the international wood pulp trade but only in a minor way because World War II effectively halted all activity at the port.

The opening of the St. Lawrence Seaway in 1958 brought an immediate upswing in local port activities. In three years Muskegon became the seventh busiest port on the Great Lakes. In one season, ninety-nine foreign ships called at the port to haul a total of 122,000 tons in overseas freight. In addition, cross-lake shipping to and from Milwaukee amounted to an annual average

Opposite page, top: *A part of the crowd of 25,000 who witnessed Whitehall's centennial parade July 6, 1960. Courtesy,* Muskegon Chronicle

Opposite page, bottom: *Lake Michigan is a lake of many temperaments. Here waves batter the Muskegon breakwater; the lighthouse is at the right. Courtesy,* Muskegon Chronicle

Right: *Among foreign imports to the Port of Muskegon were Volkswagen cars from Germany. Inspectors check this shipment in 1962. By 1969 the port was virtually shut down because of its failure to modernize. Courtesy, The Muskegon Collection, Hackley Public Library*

of more than 110,000 passengers and 700,000 tons of automobiles and other cargo.

The port reached its peak in 1962 when it handled sixty-eight different types of exports and forty-seven categories of imports. Steamship lines connected Muskegon, northern Europe, the Mediterranean, and the Far East. The exports included Brunswick bowling equipment, Continental Motors tank engines, S.D. Warren paper products, Sealed Power auto parts, Norge and Kelvinator refrigerators, Clarke floor cleaners, R.C. Allen cash registers, scrap steel from Fisher, modular homes bound for Vietnam, and frozen cherries from the Hart-Shelby area. Imports included Volkswagen and Mercedes-Benz automobiles, English clay china, Swedish steel wire, Norwegian wood pulp, and French

wine.

Yet despite this activity there was no regular service from any steamship line and the local port failed to upgrade its facilities. Eastern seaboard ports, feeling the pinch of competition from lake ports, introduced the container—a hollow metal box measuring 20 feet long, 8 feet wide, and 8 feet deep with a capacity of up to 45 tons and 2,100 cubic feet. The container offered a number of advantages, including reduced handling of shipments, fewer delays, less cargo damage, and general savings in cost and time. Containers, being of standard size, could also be easily transferred to trains and trucks.

It takes a large-scale operation to have a successful container-port, however, and Muskegon did not have the capital investment in facilities nor the high volume in shipping to compete. Many of the ships especially built to handle containers simply are too wide to fit the St. Lawrence Seaway. Weather also limits

Opposite page, left: *One of the county's forms of summer recreation is pleasure boating. Hundreds of boats are here tied up at Pointe Marine in North Muskegon's Bear Lake Channel. Courtesy,* Muskegon Chronicle

Opposite page, right: *During the winters, Lake Michigan takes on the look of the Arctic Circle. In particularly severe winters the lake will freeze almost all the way across to Milwaukee, a distance of ninety miles. Courtesy,* Muskegon Chronicle

Right: *Muskegon's Western Avenue, before it became the enclosed Muskegon Mall, was the scene of many parades. This aerial view shows the Seaway Festival parade in the early 1960s. Courtesy,* Muskegon Chronicle

use of the seaway and the Great Lakes by most ships to a season of eight or nine months.

After 1965 Muskegon rapidly lost business as shippers and ships began to use other ports. The Board of Harbor Commissioners ceased operations in 1969 after only nine years of existence. In the late 1970s the cross-lake ferry service was discontinued. It was estimated that ten million dollars was needed to make Muskegon's port competitive and no private enterprise was available to put up the capital. The beautiful harbor sits virtually idle today with only an occasional cement boat or coaler for Consumers Power's B.C. Cobb electrical plant breaking the stream of pleasure boats and salmon fishers entering or leaving the port. Public and private interests are, however, working diligently to have cross-lake ferry service reintroduced. Involved are agreements between Michigan and Wisconsin, and the cities of Muskegon and Milwaukee.

Nancy Anne Fleming of Montague, "Miss Michigan," was named Miss America in the 1960 annual pageant in Atlantic City. Since her coronation she has been a cohost of the "Lifetime" cable television show. Courtesy, Muskegon Chronicle

Above: *Modern Muskegon as it looks from Jefferson Towers. The white building in the center is the City Hall, with Urry Arch in the front. Photo by David Carlson. Courtesy, David Carlson*

Right: *The world's largest weather vane is located at the headwaters of White Lake between Whitehall and Montague. Built by Whitehall Metal Studios, the weather vane is 48 feet high and the arrow length is 26 feet, 2 inches. Photo by Richard E. Read. Courtesy, Richard E. Read*

Above and right: *The interior of the Muske-gon Museum of Art's Hackley Gallery is a sharp contrast to its Romanesque exterior. Many of the collections in the gallery, and throughout the museum, are due to the gener-osity of Charles H. Hackley. After his death in 1905, his will bequested to the Board of Edu-cation $150,000 for the purchase of "pictures of the best kind" for Muskegon. Today those pictures include paintings by Goya and Wyeth, to Picasso and Renoir. Courtesy, Muskegon Museum of Art*

Opposite page: *The Hackley Art Gallery opened June 21, 1912, the first public art gal-lery in any city or town under 30,000 in the United states. Now part of the Muskegon Mu-seum of Art, it is considered one of the finest galleries in the country. Courtesy, Muskegon Museum of Art*

Above: *This is the lower corridor of the restored Hackley House. Courtesy, Hackley Heritage Association*

Above, left: *The restored Hackley House is Muskegon's best known historical building. Built at the turn of the century, it was used for many purposes before being restored by the Hackley Heritage Association. Layers of exterior paint were removed and the original color duplicated. Many of the interior furnishings are originals. Courtesy, Hackley Heritage Association*

Left: *The library of the restored Hackley House. Courtesy, Hackley Heritage Association*

A familiar sight to all Muskegonites is the fountain in the downtown mall. The mall is unusual in that it occupies several blocks of what used to be Western Avenue, the main street. Photo by David Carlson. Courtesy, David Carlson

Above: *The Muskegon Lumberjacks of the International Hockey League staged a comeback under a new name and new management in the 1984-85 season. Muskegon has had a team in the league since 1960. Photo by David Carlson. Courtesy, David Carlson*

Right: *Water sports comprise a great deal of the Muskegon area's summer recreation. Mona Lake is one of the many inland lakes used for waterskiing, both self-propelled and by motorboat. Photo by David Carlson. Courtesy, David Carlson*

The setting sun is mirrored on a calm Lake Michigan as a group of swimmers enjoy the water. Courtesy, The Gillette Nature Center

Above: *St. Francis De Sales Catholic Church in Norton Shores is recognized nationwide as a model of modern church architecture. Photo by David Carlson. Courtesy, David Carlson*

Right: *Another of Muskegon's distinctive downtown churches is St. Mary's Catholic. The original St. Mary's was the first church built in Muskegon. Photo by David Carlson. Courtesy, David Carlson*

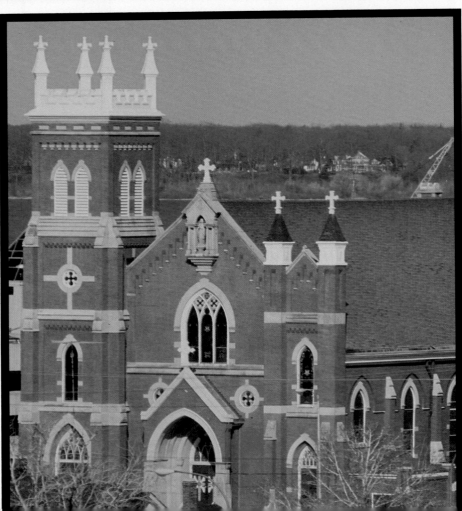

One of the hardest economic blows suffered in the Muskegon area was the 1961 move of the Norge Division of the Borg-Warner plant to Fort Smith, Arkansas, with the loss of 1,800 jobs. Courtesy, Muskegon Chronicle

In the midst of the St. Lawrence Seaway fiasco came the Vietnam War. Muskegon County contributed heavily with 5,590 men and women serving and fifty-seven casualties. Three others are still listed among the missing in action.

On top of the virtual loss of Muskegon as a port came the hard fact that the area had lost about 12,000 industrial jobs over a period of thirty years from 1952 to 1982. These included such closings as Lakey Foundry in 1972 with the loss of 1,000 jobs, and the move of Norge Division of Borg-Warner to Fort Smith, Arkansas, in 1961 with the loss of 1,800 jobs. Many factors contributed to the loss of these manufacturing jobs. These included bad labor relations (a charge widely disputed by labor leaders); Michigan workers' compensation and unemployment compensa-

tion insurance rates which were at the top or near the top of all states; high state taxes and stringent regulatory laws passed by a labor-dominated legislature.

Particularly vexing was the loss of the Norge plant which had grown out of the old Alaska Refrigeration Company, one of the original seven industries which had moved into Muskegon Heights when it was founded here before the turn of the century. The move of the Norge plant to Fort Smith cost the Muskegon area economy an estimated thirty million dollars annually.

Moves of this type, besides the plant closings, were particularly hard on the area's older workers who found it difficult or impossible to obtain new employment.

Another economic jolt was the decision by North Star Steel of St. Paul, Minnesota, to drop a bid to locate a steel mini-mill on Muskegon Lake in 1975. This evolved as a classic confrontation between the need for new jobs on one hand, opposed by environmental interests on the other.

North Star Steel even went so far as to choose Muskegon as a site for its new $50-million industrial plant in April 1975. This mini-mill was expected to employ 500 to 600 in its initial operation and potentially a total of 1,000 workers at the completion of a second rolling mill. But early in November the Cargill Corporation, parent company of North Star, announced it had

Opposite page: *The Muskegon Wastewater Management facility has become a prototype across the country. This aerial photo shows spray irrigation on crops after storage and disinfection. Courtesy,* Muskegon Chronicle

Above: *Another Muskegon landmark is "Lyon's Den," from the oldest house in Whitehall and still part of the present home. Courtesy,* Muskegon Chronicle

abandoned plans to build the mill here. Reasons given were strong opposition from a group of about 400 local residents banded together into an organization called Save our Shoreline (SOS), and delays in obtaining approval for the proposed site. The company eventually settled on Monroe, Michigan, to build its plant.

Yet a long-standing survivor of these industrial closings, the Howmet Turbine Components Corporation—opened in 1951 in Whitehall—has since become the county's largest employer. The company—originally known as MISCO—manufactures precision investment castings.

*   *   *

Despite the county's economic suffering during the recession of the early 1980s—Muskegon ranked in the top five cities in the nation for high unemployment during this period— the region recovered with the arrival of new industries and community redevelopment.

Among the industries coming to Muskegon County is the chemical industry—now viewed with mixed emotions. The Wastewater Management System gave hope that pollution could be controlled; still some twenty industrial polluters in Muskegon

Opposite page: *One of the region's most fa-mous landmarks is the blockhouse built on Horseshoe Dune overlooking Muskegon State Park and Lake Michigan. The original building was erected by the Civilian Conservation Corps in 1934. It was destroyed by arson in 1962 and was rebuilt in 1964. Courtesy,* Muskegon Chronicle

Above: *This is how the Occidental Hotel looked in 1930 before the fire of 1936 de-stroyed its ornate front. Courtesy, Charles H. Yates Collection, Muskegon County Museum*

and Ottawa counties, most of them chemical companies, have been spending millions of dollars in pollution control of ground waters and streams.

In the mid-1970s came a revolution in wastewater manage-ment in Muskegon County which is expected to become a pro-totype for areas all over the country. Wastewater from the urban areas of the county is piped away from the Lake Michigan shore-line to an inland site where it is given the equivalent of conven-tional secondary treatment. After storage and disinfection, the water with its abundance of nutrients is spray-irrigated on a vari-ety of crops. The water then passes through soil—the "living filter"—and collects in an underground drainage system, moni-tored to assure that it meets drinking water standards, and is then discharged to the surface waters of the county.

*   *   *

Besides this revolution in wastewater management, the county has witnessed a revolution of projects and developments since the 1960s.

133

Planning began in 1968 to revitalize a sagging downtown which had taken on the look of Muskegon at the end of the lumber era. In 1976 came a revolutionary change to downtown Muskegon—the Muskegon Mall. To be sure the county had several other malls, but this $15-million mall took the bulk of Muskegon's downtown business area and enclosed both sides of Western Avenue from Terrace to Third. Groundbreaking ceremonies took place November 2, 1974, and the official opening was held March 3, 1976. Sacrificed for the mall, a number of old landmarks were razed, such as the Lyman Building, Elks Temple, and the Regent Theater. Also razed was the popular Occidental Hotel to provide parking lot space on the Third Street side of the mall.

Completion of the mall triggered another ten million dollars in renovation and expansion of nearby institutions and businesses.

Above: *Muskegon's Earl Morrall gained All-America football honors at Michigan State University in 1956 and went on to a distinguished National Football League twenty-one-year career with six teams. Courtesy, Muskegon Chronicle*

Opposite page: *The old Occidental Hotel was razed in 1976 to provide parking space for the Muskegon Mall. The hotel, in one form or another, had stood for almost 100 years. Courtesy, Muskegon Chronicle*

Among the brightest prospects was the November 1984 groundbreaking for the 201-room Muskegon Harbor Hilton Hotel. Opened in the spring of 1986, the hotel amenities include a state-of-the-art convention center, banquet and restaurant facilities, and health club. The $17-million facility is located between the L.C. Walker Arena and Conference Center and the Frauenthal Center for the Performing Arts, providing a three-unit attraction center for conventions, seminars and exhibitions.

The historic Union Depot—dating back from the early 1900s—on West Western is being transformed by the Shaw-Walker Company as a showcase for their office furniture line. One of the most successful and large-scale projects is Lumbertown—a renovation of the old Breneman-Hartshorn window-shade factory. The three-story building now houses two restaurants and over thirty shops and boutiques. Under construction is a large boat sales and service complex; there are plans for a marina and waterfront park development.

Then there is Harbour Towne, underway since 1984, the complex of marine slips, (including 242 yacht slips), commercial businesses and condominiums on the old Pigeon Hill site next to the Muskegon Channel. The project is estimated to run between forty to fifty million dollars. Like Harbour Towne, the Lakeshore Yacht Harbour—opened in the spring of 1984 and developed by Cole Quality Foods, Inc.—offers sixty-two slips to private owners as "dockominiums."

In 1985 Montague applied to Coastal Zone Management for a two-phased grant to help fund a boardwalk and park improvements. A local developer received permission for a combination motel-marina complex within the shoreline area, which is expected to increase tourist activity.

*   *   *

While malls and complexes have been under construction, the county's reputation for athletic triumphs has never been lost.

Muskegon High's Earl Morrall went on to the All-American honors at Michigan State in 1956 and then enjoyed a twenty-one-year career in the National Football League with six teams, playing in the Super Bowl with the Baltimore Colts and Miami Dolphins. Muskegon Heights High School won state Class A basketball championships in 1954, 1957, and 1958 and Class B crowns in 1974, 1978, and 1979. Western Michigan Christian took state Class C basketball titles in 1958, 1962, 1965, and 1970; the Warriors also won Class C soccer crowns in 1979 and 1980 and Class D baseball title in 1985. Muskegon Catholic

One popular winter diversion on the county's small lakes is ice boating. Mona and Bear lakes are particularly suited to the speedy craft. Courtesy, *Muskegon Chronicle*

Central won state Class C football titles in 1980 and 1982.

While professional baseball died here in 1952, minor league hockey took over in 1960 to 1961 with the construction of the L.C. Walker Sports Arena. Walker, an area industrialist cut in the mold of Charles Hackley, enjoyed hockey when it was played in the old Mart in the 1930s and always said he wanted to see a facility which could handle hockey when the Mart became outmoded. He thus put up one million dollars for the arena which was built specifically for hockey and seats in excess of 5,000. Because many other uses have since been found for the building, including high school basketball games, home shows, and concerts, the arena's name was changed to the L.C. Walker Arena and Conference Center.

The late Jerry P. DeLise and his wife, Winn, brought hockey here for the 1960-61 season with the Muskegon Zephyrs in the International Hockey League. Their teams, later known as the Mohawks, won a number of season and playoff titles. DeLise sold the team in the mid-1970s to a syndicate of local professional men but the team did poorly in the box office and standings.

The club was then purchased in 1984 by Larry Gordon and, operating under the name of the Lumberjacks, was an immediate success. It won its division and finished runner-up in the post-season Turner Cup competition in its first season. The team also led the league in attendance despite having one of the smallest population areas.

Here the salmon fleet heads out of the Muskegon Channel. Courtesy, Muskegon Chronicle

Through the efforts of local outdoor sports enthusiasts and with the aid of a grant from the state, a winter sports complex is under development at Muskegon State Park. First to be built was a 600-meter Olympic-quality luge run. There are only two other luge runs in the country.

Completion of this luge run, as well as the local enthusiam and cooperation, enticed the American Athletic Union (AAU) to hold its first-ever Winter Games in Muskegon in February 1985. The AAU games included luge competition, a biathlon and cross-country skiing. The indoor events for the winter games included karate, wrestling, handball, racquetball, and ice hockey. Due to the success of the games, the AAU also held 1985 summer games in Muskegon, and the winter games once again in February 1986.

Along with the development of the sports complex, the county also plans to relocate and redevelop its county fairgrounds.

*　　　*　　　*

The county has never lost its popularity as a resort area. While vacationers in the nineteenth century came by the Goodrich Steamship Line and by railroad, today they arrive by automobile and airplane to summer in their cottages.

What looked like a disaster for the tourist business in the middle 1960s turned out to be a blessing. There is some debate whether the alewife—a trash ocean fish—entered the Great

The introduction of coho and chinook salmon in Lake Michigan has brought sportsmen from all over the country for summer fishing at Muskegon. Pictured is the Giddings Street launching ramp. Courtesy, Muskegon Chronicle

Lakes gradually over the years or in a rush due to the opening of the St. Lawrence Seaway. But suddenly there were thousands of the bony little fish piled up on the Lake Michigan shore and the stench drove bathers and tourists from the beaches.

Dr. Wayne Tody, Michigan Conservation Commission fisheries' director, introduced the coho salmon to feed on the alewife, and later stocked chinook into the lakes. Cohos were introduced into two streams in April 1966. By 1977 the salmon run was in full bloom with tourism and allied businesses increased by some 250 to 300 percent. The result was a wave of sport fishing that can hardly be surpassed anywhere in the country. Salmon weighing thirty to forty pounds are regularly caught and a charter fishing industry has developed. Now there is almost a danger that there will not be enough alewives to supply the salmon.

*   *   *

Between its strong and diverse industrial base, the popularity of its resort areas, and the many redevelopment projects, Muskegon County faces the future with promise. Throughout its history it has survived setbacks which would have surely devastated most other communities.

LEE ROOT MEMORIAL PARK:
A TINY OASIS IN THE BIG CITY

Little things which have been around for some time are sometimes overlooked in the bustle of modern living.

Such is the case with Lee Root Memorial Park which has survived since 1901 in the midst of Muskegon's bustling streets and traffic. The park, smallest in the city, is a tribute to tragic love.

This tiny park at the intersections of Muskegon, First, and Apple was donated by Mrs. Thomas Miller, who lived on Miller Avenue before it became a part of Apple Avenue.

"The memorial will commemorate a tragedy as well as serve as a tribute to a much beloved man," said Mrs. Miller, in her 1901 donation of the park.

A daughter of Mrs. Miller's, Anna, married a man named Lee Root and they lived for some time in the west wing of the Miller home at the corner of Miller and First.

"From this west wing," Mrs. Miller said, "they could look directly out on the little triangle and Mrs. Root often used to say to her husband: 'Lee, I don't believe we will ever be happier than we have been here.'

"Later, they moved to the Upper Peninsula and on October 9, 1897, at Nahma, Root was struck by a railroad train and killed. His wife was so devoted to her husband that she did not long survive him. She passed away the following March 24."

Minutes of the City Commission meetings relate:

Alderman Newton stated that Mrs. Thomas Miller desired to improve the triangle at Miller, First and Muskegon and convert it into a public park. She will lay cement walks about it and erect a fountain, her only request being that it be designated Lee

Root Memorial Park. The recorder was instructed to notify Mrs. Miller her petition and request would be honored.

The park was untouched for more than fifty years in its original form. But in 1955 a small portion had to be removed on the Muskegon and First sides for the widening of the two streets when the Norton-Glade Expressway came into downtown Muskegon.

In order to obtain the necessary eight feet of right-of-way from the park's two sides, the state had to relocate the park marker and fountain. Then-city manager George F. Liddle informed city commissioners that the park would remain intact but reduced in size. A year or so later, when the street work had been completed, the park was restored. Even the tiny cherub atop the original fountain has been replaced.

And so this miniature oasis remains today and will hopefully always remain, as a memorial to married love.

Muskegon's smallest park, Lee Root Park, stands at the intersections of Muskegon, First, and Apple. The park was donated by Mrs. Thomas Miller in honor of her son-in-law, who faced a tragic death. Courtesy, Muskegon Chronicle

Beerman's Band, organized in 1884 by Loren O. Beerman, entertained Muskegon for forty years with concerts in Hackley Park, as well as parades. This photograph shows the band in 1892, and the leader, Willard Ashley (middle row, center). Courtesy, Charles H. Yates Collection, Muskegon County Museum

7 *Partners in Progress*

Business began on the banks of Muskegon County's waterways more than 150 years ago, even before the city's name was adopted. Upon reflection, the community's economic history could best be described as interesting—boom to bust and back again—but never boring.

Historians say French fur trader Jean Recollect Baptista established Muskegon County's first trading post in 1812 near the mouth of Bear Lake Channel. The trading of traps, guns, and whisky for animal pelts brought in by Ottawa, Chippewa, and Potawatomia Indians ended in the 1830s.

About the same time white pioneers began to build sawmills on the Muskegon Lake flats. The city earned the title Lumber Queen as a result of fifty years of sawing pine and hardwood timbers and boards. Much of the lumber was used in rebuilding Chicago after the Great Fire. At that time Muskegon was a real port city, shipping lumber across Lake Michigan in sailing schooners.

Lumbering reached a peak in the 1880s. As it faded the city moved into the industrial age. Lumber magnates Charles Hackley and Thomas Hume, as well as other business leaders, were not averse to luring industries to Muskegon from Chicago, Milwaukee, and other Midwest cities.

Manufacturing armaments to fight two world wars and two Asian conflicts provided additional periods of prosperity and earned the community the name Arsenal of Democracy. The Great Depression took its toll but fostered new businesses as underemployed or jobless workmen turned to entrepreneurship to feed themselves and their families.

In the early decades of the twentieth century, Muskegon became the car and truck motor capital of the world. Auxiliary manufacturing also made the region the machine shop and pattern-making center of Michigan and the Midwest.

An oil boom in the 1920s and a flirtation with international shipping through the St. Lawrence Seaway, which brought on the "Port City" title in the 1950s, were both short-lived. States in the Midwest and Sun Belt began to lure away manufacturers in the 1960s. The auto industry recession of the early 1980s cut further into employment.

Some manufacturing losses have been offset economically by the development of regional retailing centers such as the Muskegon Mall, as well as growth of the health care and education industries, and state, county, and municipal construction projects. As community leaders look to the future, they are actively promoting projects to develop the lakeshore's potential for tourism and recreation.

The organizations whose stories are detailed on the following pages have chosen to support this important literary and civic project. They illustrate the variety of ways in which individuals and their businesses have contributed to the area's growth and development. The civic involvement of Muskegon County's businesses, learning institutions, and local government, as well as its citizens, has made the region an excellent place to live and work.

MUSKEGON AREA CHAMBER OF COMMERCE

Muskegon business leaders have been organized to promote community development for more than a century. Organizational names and personnel have changed over the years, but the basic purpose remains the same: to assist business owners individually and the community as a whole.

The Board of Trade was organized in 1884 and within five years had attracted four new industries to the city. The Muskegon Development Company was formed in the late 1890s to develop what was to become the city of Muskegon Heights and to foster new industry within its borders. Both the Board of Trade and The Muskegon Development Company were responsible for attracting new industry from other cities and helping local residents get started in the manufacturing industry.

The Muskegon Chamber of Commerce was first organized in 1915. By 1928 it had been renamed the Greater Muskegon Chamber of Commerce. Three years later businessmen organized the Muskegon Progress and Development Fund in an effort to overcome a Depression-troubled economy.

In 1964 the organization became the Muskegon Area Chamber of Commerce and Development Council, which is essentially its structure today. The chamber and affiliated organizations that make up the Muskegon Area Center for Business, Industry, and Tourism are housed in the

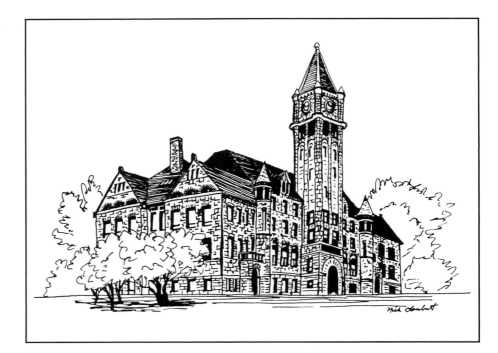

The Muskegon Area Center for Business, Industry and Tourism is located at 349 West Webster Avenue.

Muskegon Public Schools' administration building at Webster Avenue and Fourth Street.

Currently the chamber operates three programs under contract: the Convention and Visitors' Bureau of Muskegon County, On-the-Job Training, and Federal Procurement Assistance. Cooperating groups include New Muskegon and its

Aerial photo of downtown Muskegon.

Muskegon-Oceana outreach effort, the labor management committee, the Muskegon County Economic Development Corporation, and SCORE (Service Corps of Retired Executives). The Women's Division is an allied, autonomous organization.

Much of the organization's work involving its various programs is carried out by its members serving on committees. The prominently active committees include Business After Hours, Legislative Action, ambassadors, transportation, Chemical Council, Political Action, and small business.

Today membership in the Muskegon Area Chamber of Commerce represents a wide range of businesses. Categories range from amusement/entertainment to wholesale/distributors and include automotive, construction/contractors, individuals/nonprofit agencies, financial, hotels/motels/apartments, insurance/real estate, manufacturers/processors, professional, public utilities, publishers/printers, radio/television, restaurants/cafés/taverns, retail business/personal services, and transportation.

HUNTER-HUGHES, INC.

This was the first shop of Hunter Brothers Plumbing & Heating on First Street at Clay Avenue. Pictured are (left to right) Matthew Dwyer, George Hepburn, Bertha DeLong, and brothers Harry K. and Alfred J. Hunter. Photo circa 1913

In 1912 Alfred J. Hunter and Harry K. Hunter started Hunter Bros., a plumbing company that eventually became the present Hunter-Hughes, Inc. The firm was located on First Street, where the Muskegon Federal Savings & Loan building now stands. In 1915 Hunter Bros. moved to the corner of Western and Terrace streets, and four years later, to 252 Market Street. In 1922 Alfred Hunter purchased Harry Hunter's share of the business and the company became Alfred J. Hunter & Co. The company remained at 252 Market Street until after World War II, when it moved to its present location on Henry Street in 1946.

Over the years Hunter & Co. furnished much of the material required for the residential and industrial growth of Muskegon. One of the firm's early contracts was to furnish the piping and valve requirements for the *General C.B. Sears,* a U.S. Department of Engineers tugboat that plied the Great Lakes for many years before World War I. As Muskegon grew industrially, so did Hunter & Co.

Malcolm W. Hughes, a graduate mechanical engineer from the University of Michigan, joined the company in 1944 after spending eleven years with the Shaw-Walker Co. of Muskegon. His plant engineering experience and technical background were of great value to the firm at a time when the chemical industry was becoming a major factor in the industrial growth of Muskegon.

Hughes became company president in 1959. Hunter, his father-in-law, remained as board chairman until his retirement in 1966. At that time Hughes and his wife, Jane, became sole owners of the organization. Hughes remained as president and board chairman until his retirement in 1977. At that time a controlling interest in the company was bought by a group of key employees, and Robert Morin, Sr., became president and board chairman.

Morin is a former mayor of Roosevelt Park and has served two years as president of the Muskegon Area Chamber of Commerce. His background includes serving with the Seabees in northern Africa and plant engineering work with the Anaconda Wire & Cable Co. of Muskegon.

To reflect new ownership and emphasize the change from plumbing to industrial supply sales, the company's name was changed to Hunter-Hughes, Inc., in 1975.

The firm now occupies 50,000 square feet of modern office and warehouse space in Muskegon and a 7,500-square-foot branch operation in Ludington, Michigan. Hunter-Hughes, Inc., is a major supplier of process and control equipment to western Michigan industry. It is also a major supplier of irrigation and related equipment to the state's resort areas. It fabricates snowmaking equipment that has been shipped to ski areas as far away as Alaska, South America, and Japan.

Hunter-Hughes, Inc., has entered the computer age with a background buried in the early history of Muskegon, and a friendly relationship with its customers and the Muskegon community. It intends to keep this relationship alive as it contributes to the growth of greater Muskegon and western Michigan.

By 1920 the Hunter brothers had moved their plumbing store to 252 Market Street. In the picture display area are (from left) Clara B. Hodapp, Alfred J. Hunter, Harry Hunter, and John Neil, shop foreman.

TELEDYNE CONTINENTAL MOTORS GENERAL PRODUCTS

America's love affair with the horseless carriage was only a modest blush when Muskegon lured a new engine manufacturing firm into moving across Lake Michigan from Chicago. As the romance of motoring blossomed, the company matured into Teledyne Continental Motors, Muskegon's leading employer for a half-century.

Ross W. Judson fathered the firm. Fresh out of college, in 1902 he began building internal-combustion engines in a small Chicago machine shop. Financial aid from relatives enabled him to build more motors, move to larger quarters, and found Autocar Equipment Company.

As the lumber era faded into history, Muskegon city government and business leaders got voters to approve a $200,000 bond issue to help attract new industry to the area. As a result, Muskegon scored a big coup on July 5, 1905, when Judson signed a contract with the Muskegon Chamber of Commerce to bring Continental Motors Manufacturing Company to town.

A two-story brick factory at Market and Water streets went up quickly, and production began May 15, 1906.

Built in 1942, the Getty Street plant has housed Teledyne Continental Motors tank and aircraft engine facilities. It was designated as TCM General Products Division in the mid-1970s.

Ross Judson, founder, established Continental Motors Manufacturing Company in Muskegon in 1905.

One of the first important orders called for Continental to build 100 engines, one per day, for Studebaker Wagon Company of South Bend, Indiana. Other early automobiles powered by Continental's engines were Auburn, Hudson, Jordan, Paige-Detroit, Saxon, Velie, Davis, and Moon.

Soon Continental bought adjoining property and expanded its factory space. The firm had far exceeded an employment bonus clause in its contract, and in 1919 the city deeded to Continental the original factory site. A car with a Continental engine won one of the early Indianapolis races, boosting the firm's reputation.

Dispersion from Muskegon began in 1909 when Hudson Motor Company ordered 10,000 engines. That led Judson to sign a long-term contract and build a factory near Hudson's Detroit plant. By 1916 Continental had 2,100 men turning out nearly 300 engines per day for many of the nation's small car manufacturers.

With the United States furnishing France and England with war vehicles, Continental's entire Muskegon production in early 1917 consisted of

One of Ross Judson's first engines is a museum piece.

truck and ambulance motors. Military production spurted when the United States entered World War I. Later Continental officials refinanced the firm and rechartered it under Virginia law as Continental Motors Corporation (CMC).

Engine demand dropped during the postwar business slump. Automakers, especially General Motors, Ford, and Chrysler, were designing and building their own engines. CMC moved to diversify its business, manufacturing engines for farm equipment and heavy construction machinery.

William Angell, a Muskegon lawyer and CMC stockholder, was made

president in 1930. During his tenure he moved the company toward building its own automobiles and expanding aircraft engine production. The three-model line of Continental cars was short-lived, but the airplane engines were to carry the firm into the jet age.

Clarence "Jack" Reese took the company helm in 1939. A hard-driving worker, he made Continental a leader in the construction of vehicle and aircraft engines. Continental Aviation and Engineering (CAE) was formed in 1940 to consolidate aircraft engine research and development.

Engine production soared as Europe warred again. As a result, the United States government ordered more armaments to help the Allies fight Nazi Germany. In 1942 the U.S. Defense Plant Corporation financed the building and equipping of a new factory on Getty Street, adjacent to the city of Muskegon. CAE moved in quickly to produce parts and then entire engines for pursuit and bomber planes. The Market Street plant also turned out engines for tanks, trucks, and other military vehicles.

William Angell headed Continental Motors in the 1930s.

C.J. "Jack" Reese led CMC to prominence during World War II and the Korean War.

In 1944, at the peak of World War II, Continental employed 11,000 workers. A quarter of the employees were women, who replaced men drafted into the armed services. A major breakthrough came about when CMC engineers tried a nine-cylinder aircraft engine in a U.S. Army medium tank. It worked. And, as a result, thousands were manufactured for United States and Allied armored units.

After the war CMC resumed making engines for trucks, buses, Kaiser-Frazer cars, and Checker taxicabs. When Continental marked its fiftieth anniversary in 1952, its people had built 7,000 engines for cars and trucks.

When U.S. troops were ordered into Korea, CMC stepped up tank engine production, and the Getty Street plant's work force reached 5,000 in 1953. Later, peace in Korea brought military cutbacks. However, the interstate highway program enacted by congress in 1954 created a demand for heavy construction engines.

Ryan Aeronautical Company of San Diego completed a stock-purchase takeover of Continental in 1966. Ryan's G.W. "Bill" Rutherford replaced Reese as president in 1966. Three years later Teledyne, Inc., a Los Angeles-based conglomerate, purchased Ryan and Continental.

Teledyne Continental Motors was split into five operating divisions in 1972. Harold W. Rouse, who began his career with Ryan, moved up to president of TCM General Products Division on Getty Street in 1974. He managed the firm through further refining and building of tank engines and combat vehicles.

In 1984 Thomas J. Keenan succeeded Rouse as president of TCM General Products. The company currently employs 900 people, who build air-cooled diesel tank engines and modernize existing armored tracked units for the U.S. Army and the armed forces of the Free World nations.

TCM Industrial Products' Market Street plant produces gasoline engines for agriculture, construction, and industrial equipment. Teledyne CAE, located in Toledo, Ohio, manufactures turbojet engines for missiles and remote-piloted vehicles. TCM Aircraft Products, Mobile, Alabama, produces light aircraft engines for the general aviation industry.

Thomas J. Keenan became TCM General Products president in 1984.

Much of the historical data and some of the photos for this biography are excerpts from the book Continental! Its Motors and Its People, by William Wagner, published in 1983. The author's permission to use the material is gratefully acknowledged.

GEERPRES, INC.

An old adage says, "Invent a better mousetrap, and the world will beat a path to your door." Elmer Bard saw a greater need to improve the mop wringer of his day rather than the mousetrap. As a result, he began making wringers and, instead of waiting for the world to come to him, loaded a week's output into his 1931 Oldsmobile and sold them door to door to Muskegon businessmen.

It was 1935, well into the Great Depression, when Bard began work in one small room on the second floor of a former horse stable. He had purchased the patent for a cast-iron mop wringer and redesigned it to be made from welded steel parts. Fifty years later Geerpres, Inc., has grown into one of the leading U.S. companies furnishing equipment and supplies to the commercial building maintenance industry.

Today Geerpres employs forty-seven people at its modern plant on Harvey Street and Laketon Avenue. Workers assemble mop handles, wringers, buckets, sprayers, and carts from parts manufactured by western Michigan firms. This equipment and a varied line of cleaning accessories are marketed worldwide through a

The modern plant and offices of Geerpres, Inc., are located at the intersection of US 31 and Laketon Avenue.

network of sales representatives. Douglas C. Bard, one of Elmer's sons, serves as chairman with his partner, John F. "Jack" Tierney, president and chief executive officer.

There was a reason Elmer Bard sold a week's production of his mop wringers at a time. Money was extremely scarce in the depressed 1930s, and he needed the cash from one week's sales to buy more steel to make wringers the next week. It was classic supply-side economics. Bard's customers were people who ran stores, shops, and restaurants. Those small businessmen usually cleaned their own floors after closing for the day. "They couldn't turn me down," Bard once said. "A purchase meant more free time to spend at home with their families."

Geerpres sustained its first setback the second year Bard was in business. Customers began to return the wringers because the gear teeth were disengaging. However, that complaint proved to be a blessing in disguise. Bard claimed that a divine inspiration instructed him to use the original gear system but stagger the teeth in two rows. This solved the problem.

Business grew, more products were added, and the company took over all of the stable's second floor. Further growth prompted a move to a converted church on Diana Avenue. When World War II began, the War Production Board refused to allocate steel for cleaning equipment. Geerpres survived by machining small

parts and plating large artillery recoil springs after adding a plating department. Peacetime was highlighted by four additions to the Harvey Street plant and by the manufacture of the first stainless steel buckets, larger and improved wringers, and housekeeping carts.

Douglas Bard has worked at Geerpres since 1953. During the mid- and late 1950s he and his brother, Herbert, were the only sales force. They divided the country, setting up distribution nationwide. In 1966 the Bard family sold the business to Beatrice Foods. Elmer Bard continued as an engineering and sales adviser until shortly before his death in 1978 at the age of eighty-eight. Geerpres, Inc., returned to local ownership when Douglas Bard and Jack Tierney bought it from Beatrice in 1983.

Elmer H. Bard holds the first Geerpres wringer model produced by his company.

Elmer H. Bard began manufacturing Geerpres mop wringers in one room on the second floor of this former stable at 51 Clay Street.

LAKESHORE MACHINERY & SUPPLY CO.

"Service with a smile" has proved to be the touchstone of success for Lakeshore Machinery & Supply Co. and the people who have run it for a half-century.

From the time he purchased a Depression-foundering machine repair business in 1934, Arnold G. Andersen practiced the concept of total customer service and urged his colleagues and employees to do the same. He once told a trade magazine writer: "Service is the thing we are all going to have to provide more of. No longer can a distributor offer just warehouse space and good deliveries to his customers. He has to really take care of customer needs."

Andersen was president of the firm until 1968, when he was elevated to board chairman, a position he actively held until his death in 1984. His credo of service carries on through his son, Roger A. Andersen, company president since 1968, the management team, and all employees.

Today Lakeshore's three operating companies—industrial supply, machine tool, and material handling—and corporate offices are housed at 450 West Hackley Avenue, in Muskegon. Each company sells and services industrial supplies and equipment through branches in Kalamazoo, Grand Rapids, and Traverse City. They further offer customers computerized teleprocessing of orders,

Arnold G. Andersen started his business in this building at 1922 Peck Street.

analysis of their work systems, a fleet of delivery and service trucks, and training in new processes and new equipment operation.

Peninsular Investment, a separate corporation, makes Lakeshore different from most industrial distributors. It provides financing for tools and equipment to help fledgling companies get off the ground.

Lakeshore's story began during the Great Depression. While managing the E.H. Sheldon Company furniture factory, Andersen began working evenings and weekends with others who had taken over the faltering Lakeshore Corporation, founded in 1922 at 1922 Peck Street. He acquired controlling interest in 1934, and six years later moved the business to larger quarters at 400 West Laketon Avenue.

In 1954 the firm acquired the

Hackley Street site and consolidated all its Muskegon operations there ten years later. The 1960s, 1970s, and early 1980s were marked by additions to the home plant and the acquisition of firms in Muskegon, Grand Rapids, and Kalamazoo. On January 1, 1986, Lakeshore Machinery & Supply Co. became three distinct companies each with increased employee ownership. Roger Andersen heads Lakeshore Industrial Supply, Inc.; Robert Weisse, Lakeshore Machinery, Inc.; and Kenneth Babcock, Lakeshore Material Handling, Inc.

Arnold Andersen served his community, church, and family as well as his company. He encouraged several new business ventures, served as a chamber of commerce director and North Muskegon city councilman, headed the draft board during World War II, received the Boy Scouts' Silver Beaver Award, and worked to build the present First Congregational Church while serving as a trustee.

Roger Andersen's record of community service includes time spent as chamber of commerce director and chairman of INDEX, the organization's industrial expansion committee; twelve years as Hackley Hospital director, six as chairman of the board; Muskegon County Community Foundation Board chairman; director of New Muskegon; and trustee of the First Congregational Church.

The three Lakeshore companies operate from these facilities at 450 West Hackley Avenue in Muskegon.

HACKLEY HOSPITAL

Charles H. Hackley would probably not recognize his hospital were the lumber baron-philanthropist able to return to Muskegon. Hackley Hospital's growth during its first eighty years reflects the phenomenal development of the nation's health care industry, not only in buildings and equipment but also in personnel and their ability to heal the ill and injured.

Both the Muskegon *Chronicle* and the *Morning News* described in detail dedication proceedings for the new institution on November 17, 1904. Schools, banks, and businesses closed at noon. Townspeople and guests listened to dignitaries orate and an orchestra play for the formal program in the Grand Theater and Opera House. Most of the 6,000 attending rode streetcars and horse-drawn carriages from the theater to walk through and view the new hospital on the southeast corner of town.

During the ceremony Harry Sawyer, one of the trustees, said that Hackley had doubled his original gift of two blocks of land so that architects would not have to cramp the three-story building's style. Sawyer

also stated that the benefactor's gift had swelled from $75,000 to $200,000 for land, building, and equipment. Hackley's gift assured Muskegon the most modern hospital of its time.

Today Hackley Hospital continues this tradition. The original building has been replaced by a four-wing structure through remodeling, renovation, and expansion.

The central wing houses radiology, laboratory, physiology, a sleep clinic, and radiation therapy. The south wing contains pediatrics, orthopedics, and inpatient rehabilitation. The first floor of the north wing houses administration, inpatient surgery, and a large outpatient surgery area. The second floor is dedicated to obstetrics with a new birthing room and family-oriented classes. The fifth floor is an inpatient cancer treatment floor with isolation units and a specially trained staff. The east wing houses intensive and cardiac care units, and medical/surgical floors.

A nursing program was started in 1905, and a school, built thirteen years later, was expanded twice. Nurses' training was shifted to Muskegon Community College in 1982. A year later the renovated school building was converted into the Hackley Health Resources Center, containing business offices and com-

Today the hospital continues to serve the Muskegon area with the newest technology and a caring environment.

munity services, and serving as home to the American Cancer Society, Arthritis Foundation, and Senior Services of Muskegon.

Northwood Center is an award-winning, inpatient psychiatric facility located on the hospital grounds. The Professional Center houses physicians' offices, the Hackley Pharmacy, West Michigan Healthcare Equipment Company, and the only occupational health clinic in the region. A sports medicine clinic is also located in the Professional Center. Dr. Frank Garber, one of the first trustees, admitted the first patient, Mrs. Frederick Collins of North Muskegon, one day after the dedication in 1904.

Today Gordon A. Mudler is the hospital's president and the administrator of its ninety-five departments. In 1985 Hackley had a licensed capacity of 358 beds and averaged 11,000 admissions per year. The staff of 160 doctors was supported by 1,100 full- and part-time employees.

Hackley Hospital's outstanding list of services includes a cancer treatment center and a laser center for a variety of surgeries performed with the high-energy light beam. The institution also fosters support groups for patients and their families in such fields as diabetes, weight control, health and wellness, and stress management.

Hackley Hospital was given to Muskegon in 1902 and dedicated in 1904 to provide for "the relief of the sick and suffering, and the promotion of medical science."

HOLCOMB REPORTING SERVICE, INC.

Holcomb Reporting Service, Inc., a court-reporting agency organized in 1953, was at that time a unique business venture in western Michigan. Although there were independent free-lancing court reporters working in the area, there was no entity capable of efficiently meeting the reporting requirements of the legal community. Thus HRS, Inc., was born.

The founder of the corporation, Marguerite Holcomb, was the first woman in Muskegon County to enter the then all-male field of court reporting in the area. She was appointed official circuit court reporter of the county, one of six women in Michigan to serve in that capacity.

Following the demise of circuit court Judge Joseph F. Sanford, she turned to free-lance reporting. Recognizing the need for an orderly method of furnishing reporters for taking depositions, reporting testimony in various courts and governmental agencies, she established the present free-lance agency. In 1954 the fledgling company procured a contract from the State of Michigan for reporting all workmen's compensation hearings throughout western Michigan; and the present thriving business still holds that contract.

This small but vital service company has grown to about thirty employees. Besides the eleven-room commercial building depicted here, a building next door was acquired and two downstairs apartments were converted into additional office space.

Although Mrs. Holcomb is what is termed in the profession as a "pen writer" utilizing Gregg shorthand, the company's modern writers use machine shorthand to attain the necessary speed of 225 words per minute that all certified reporters must have.

The latest innovation in the court-reporting profession is the CAT (computer-assisted transcript), where the stenograph notes of a court reporter are fed into the computer and are transcribed into typewritten form. The CAT system replaces the time-consuming process of the reporter dictating his/her notes and an operator typing the dictation. If needed, courtroom testimony can now be instantaneously printed for judge, jury, or attorneys. Also, the inefficient tape recorder experiment can now join the horse-and-buggy era.

Mrs. Holcomb still takes pride in an idea of hers that resulted in the redesigning of a typewriter keyboard for court reporting. She worked with IBM to place *Q, A,* and *?* in lower-case mode so these symbols could be typed without using the shift key at the beginning or end of almost every line. This innovation was listed as the "court reporter's keyboard" in the IBM brochure for over thirty years, and used by most reporters in the country.

The motto of HRS, Inc., "Have shorthand, will travel," and its reputation of expertise in reporting medical and technical testimony, led Mrs. Holcomb and some of her reporters to jobs in far-flung places such as San Diego, Los Angeles, San Francisco, Houston, Milwaukee, Chicago, Boston, New York, and Pittsburgh, and Mrs. Holcomb herself spent five days in London, England, taking medical depositions.

While pursuing her career, Mrs. Holcomb raised three children: a daughter who has her own court-reporting business in York, Pennsylvania; a son who is a board-certified physician; and a daughter who is a student in commercial design.

Ten years ago Mrs. Holcomb entered politics. Her concern for city economic policies, and her reputation as an able businesswoman, won her a seat on the Muskegon City Commission, making her the first woman ever to attain that position. Fellow commissioners elected her vice-mayor her third year in office, then selected her the first female mayor of Muske-

Marguerite Holcomb, the county's first female official court reporter, achieved many honors in her illustrious career, including serving as mayor of Muskegon in 1980 and 1981.

gon in 1980 and 1981.

Other activities have been varied. She is past state president of the Michigan Shorthand Reporters Association, and past state president of Michigan Business & Professional Women's Clubs; was named Michigan Small Businesswoman in 1969; and locally, she was named Woman of the Year in 1970 and Entrepreneur of the Year in 1984.

Mrs. Holcomb's present service includes acting as a Muskegon Area Chamber of Commerce board member, OJT committee chairman in the Job Training & Partnership Act program, president of the chamber's Women's Division, and twelve years of membership in the United Way. She is listed in *Who's Who of American Women.*

Holcomb Reporting Service, Inc., registered professional court reporters, serves the western Michigan legal field from this 1891 Lakeshore Drive location.

COLE'S QUALITY FOODS, INC.

Bread and boats. That is the story of Cole's Quality Foods, Inc., and Lakeshore Yacht Harbor, two growing enterprises on Lakeshore Drive a few blocks from downtown Muskegon.

Cole's is emerging as a major company in the frozen-food industry by concentrating on the production and marketing of a single product—frozen garlic bread.

Lakeshore Yacht Harbor, Cole's wholly owned subsidiary, lies at the base of the bluff on which the firm's corporate offices and bakery are located. The Muskegon Lake harbor site was a vacant sandbank in early 1983. Today it offers modern marina facilities and soon will add waterfront condominium town houses.

This story began August 9, 1943, when L. Carroll Cole purchased the Cruikshank Bakery at 2534 Peck Street in Muskegon Heights. Bread, rolls, and pastries were sold at the front of the small building. Carroll's brother, H. Hubert Cole, joined the business in 1945.

Carroll Cole recalls that the bakery's first retail outlet was in Grossman's Department Store; the second was in the city's bus terminal. After World War II sugar rationing ended, the firm began to move its wares to supermarket shelves. Cole saw the advantage of one-stop shopping and

Cole's Quality Foods' corporate office building of the future. The new structure will adjoin the existing automated bakery and freezer facilities.

opened more supermarket outlets during the postwar boom.

Business growth prompted a move from Peck Street to a larger plant at Glade Street and Grand Avenue in 1950. To keep up with growing demand, production began in a renovated and remodeled former brewery building at 1188 Lakeshore Drive in 1977. Today that structure houses the firm's production facility and corporate offices.

By the late 1970s more than 100 varieties of fresh bakery goods were being sold in seventy Michigan supermarkets. However, high production costs forced a decision by Wes Devon to close the retail division and concentrate on the frozen product. Since that decision Cole's has experienced dramatic and profitable growth.

Cole's microwave garlic loaf is the bakery industry's first product that can be heated in microwave ovens. Cole's products are sold in all fifty states and at U.S. military bases worldwide.

Cole regularly visits the plant and offices in his capacity as special consultant. Active in the Rotary Club and foreign student exchange program, he was honored as Muskegon Man of the Year in 1985 for his contributions to community improvement.

Wesley S. Devon, who had joined the company in 1972 as marketing vice-president, became chief executive officer in 1981. Devon has devoted his time and energies to corporate growth through expansion of production and sales development of Cole's as an international company. He has backed community growth through new job development and the expansion of the area's recreation and housing facilities via Lakeshore Yacht Harbor.

Ground was broken in November 1983 for the marina/condominium complex. It is the area's first marine recreation development to open in recent years. Harbor features include sixty-three slips for sailboat and powerboat owners, utility and fuel services, a members' lounge and service building, and a family recreation area.

Lakeshore Yacht Harbor offers waterfront living for sixty-three boat owners. Condominium town houses will be built nearby.

KAYDON CORPORATION

Machines that are stationary and those that move underground, across land and water, through the air, and in space all need bearings for continued motion and mobility.

The people of Kaydon Corporation have produced such bearings since the company's inception at the outset of World War II. By 1985 total production of the many sizes and shapes of precision bearings numbered in the billions.

A. Harold Frauenthal had been engineering precision machinery in South Bend, Indiana, when he moved to Muskegon in 1941 and founded Kaydon. The plant erected at 2860 McCracken Street, then Norton Township, was the first in the Muskegon area designed solely for war production. Kaydon's first major job was the manufacture of bearings for Bofors gun mounts on Navy warships. No other U.S. bearing company would take on the task of producing fifty-inch and larger Bofors bearings.

Kaydon turns out custom-designed, high-precision bearings for manufacturers of industrial and military equipment. The firm operates seven plants, three in Muskegon and one each in Newaygo, Michigan; Sumter, South Carolina; Greeneville, Tennessee; and LaGrange, Georgia. In the mid-1980s over 600 of Kaydon's 930 employees worked in the Muskegon facilities.

Kaydon has gained world leadership in producing thin, cross-sectioned bearings for high-technology instruments and machines. Workers wearing surgery-type masks and clothing perform the final operation on some types of bearings in the "White Room." There jewel-like bearings are protected from bacteria and dust particles larger than 200 microns (200 one-thousandths of a millimeter).

Ball bearings from one inch to geared models measuring 180 inches in diameter go into motorized vehi-

cles ranging from mining machines to space shuttles and satellites. Roller bearings are produced for diverse customer applications including jet plane landing gears, oil field machinery, and other heavy-duty equipment. Filters that keep impurities out of hydraulic fluids, jet engines, and diesel fuel are manufactured at the firm's plants in LaGrange, Georgia, and Greeneville, Tennessee.

The McCracken Street site houses corporate offices and bearing manufacturing facilities. The original plant has been expanded several times, and the automotive plant is on the same site. The precision machining plant on Estes Street in Muskegon Industrial Park was built in 1979.

Muskegonites remember Frauenthal for his community contributions through the Frauenthal Foundation, which bought the downtown Michigan Theater to save it from destruction. The ornate 1920s movie palace and adjacent buildings now form the Frauenthal Center for the Performing Arts.

Frauenthal sold Kaydon to Commercial Credit Company in 1942 to generate financing for military production. Keene Corporation acquired Kaydon in 1969, the year both Frauenthal and Frank Donovan, another founder and the company's

Born of a need to produce naval warship gunmount bearings during World War II, Kaydon Corporation is still producing precision bearings and is headquartered in these offices on McCracken Street, Norton Shores.

first president, retired. The firm then passed through ownership by Bairnco and several managers before becoming a public stock corporation in 1984. Today Kaydon Corporation is operated by Richard A. Shantz of Muskegon, who serves as president, and Glen W. Bailey of New York, chairman of the board.

Heavy-duty mining and construction machines, such as cranes, rotate on huge bearings precision machined by Kaydon Corporation technicians.

AMERICAN COIL SPRING COMPANY

The American Coil Spring factory as originally built in Muskegon in 1928.

Springs. We use many each day, but are not conscious of the varied tasks they perform to make our work easier and our life a little smoother.

The people of American Coil Spring Company know springs inside out, upside down, and sideways. They design, engineer, manufacture, and market more than 6,000 different types of springs, wire forms, and stamped products. Of American Coil Spring's 300 employees, 105 had completed 25 or more years of service in 1985, and the average for all employees was 23.6 years.

Springmaking is a highly competitive business. American Coil Spring ranks among the top 3 percent of the nation's 700 springmakers in terms of its size. From the original concept popularly known as "winding wire on a broomstick," American Coil Spring has grown into the most diversified springmaker in the United States.

Robert Voyt, company president, said American Coil Spring's high ranking stems from the cooperative spirit of employees and management and their collective expertise developed in over sixty years of springmaking.

American Coil Spring produced 800 million springs in 1985, the greatest number of which went to the automotive industry. To illustrate the importance of the automotive market to the spring industry, an average car contains over 2,000 springs. They function in such components as carburetors, engines, transmissions, door locks, seat controls, windshield washer motors, manual and power window lifts, glove compartments, and sun visors.

Electric and electronic home appliances make up the next-largest market for American Coil Spring's products. Other applications include farm tractors and implements, construction and building equipment, electrical conductors and circuit breakers, typewriters, toys, telephone switching equipment, and recoil starters for small engines, such as those used on lawn mowers.

The firm was founded in Chicago by brothers Albert and Edward Bitzer. They purchased another Chicago spring steel company and incorporated as American Coil Spring in 1923. The new business then absorbed an additional Chicago firm to acquire its own heat-treating capability. Edward purchased Albert's interest four years later and decided to build a plant in Muskegon to be closer to the growing automotive industry.

The Greater Muskegon Industrial Foundation arranged financial assistance, and work was begun in 1928

Employee Darryl Yonkers operates a modern spring coiler.

American Coil Spring workers unload material and prepare to load barrels of springs onto the company truck in 1933.

to build a factory on Keating Avenue. The plant site was in the Foundation's industrial subdivision in what was then Muskegon Township. Shortly after construction began, the partially erected structure was destroyed by a severe storm. It was rebuilt and production started several months later. Sixty people were employed at the Chicago and Muskegon plants at that time.

As the Great Depression worsened, Bitzer decided to close the Chicago plant. However, determined efforts of both the owners and employees kept the Muskegon factory going through that business-stifling era.

Production shifted to war material soon after December 7, 1941. Many women joined the firm's growing work force. Postwar production prospered, and the factory was expanded and new equipment added.

Following Edward Bitzer's death in 1958, another brother, Harry Bitzer, became president. Michael Voyt, who had been vice-president and plant manager, headed the firm after Harry's death in 1973. Michael retired in 1975, turning American Coil Spring over to his son, Robert, who had started with the business in 1956

as a sales engineer.

In 1979 a subsidiary, Carolina Spring Company, was established in Anderson, South Carolina, to broaden the firm's marketing base and provide specialized manufacturing. Carolina Spring accounted for about 5 percent of the parent company's 1985 sales volume.

"The growth and success of American Coil Spring are attributed to one of our most valued and appreciated assets—the dedication and craftsmanship of our people," Voyt says.

While guiding American Coil Spring Company to continued suc-

Offices and main entrance to the American Coil Spring Company plant, which has been expanded several times.

cess, Robert Voyt has devoted time and energy to various community endeavors. He has been a director of the United Way and chairman of its industrial division, past president of Junior Achievement and the Muskegon Manufacturers' and Employers' Association, and director of the Muskegon Community Catholic Foundation. He has also served on a special committee that was formed to study and recommend improvements in the Muskegon County educational system.

Employee Carroll Young measures the outside diameter of a spring.

CLYDE HENDRICK REALTORS

As a young man trying to earn a living in western Michigan, Clyde Hendrick made an unusual change in occupation: He switched from hauling foundry sand and cinders with horses and wagons and entered the real estate business.

Over a period of years Hendrick's knack for negotiating property sales became the basis for one of Muskegon's leading realty firms. Today the two Clyde Hendrick real estate offices are operated by his son, Robert, and son-in-law, Gerald Jett. They learned the business and how it was built firsthand from the founder.

In the early 1900s, before real estate was even a dream, Hendrick loaded sand at the Mona Lake pits near his family farm and hauled it to foundries such as Campbell, Wyant & Cannon, and Enterprise Brass. Returning, he carted used casting sand or cinders from smelting ore and dumped them into mud holes and ruts on Norton Township dirt roads and farm lanes. Soon farmers began to ask if he knew of someone who might want to buy their land or if he knew of another farm for sale. Occasionally he was able to bring buyer and seller together and close a deal.

After World War I he quit wagon-

Clyde Hendrick founded the Muskegon real estate firm that still bears his name.

eering and started brokering farms full time. Hendrick's partner wanted him to work on Sunday when farmers were at home. He refused and went out on his own. He obtained a state license and began listing western Michigan farms from Benton Harbor to Manistee.

In the mid-1920s Hendrick opened his first office in the Danigelis building on Broadway and Peck streets in Muskegon Heights. His sister, Emma, was the first office secretary. Another sister, Mae, soon joined them in the business.

The young broker undertook a major job at the request of the county supervisors board, securing options on property that became Muskegon International Airport. He also helped obtain the sites for Hoffmaster State Park and Muskegon General Hospital.

He developed part of the Hendrick family farm into Brookside, the area's first subdivision. Brookside, Lake Harbor Estates, Dorset Meadows, and the Greenfield Estates housing developments, which were platted later, formed the residential nucleus for the south portion of the city of Nor-

ton Shores.

Hendrick's business boomed. In 1957 he constructed and moved into a new office at 2301 Peck. The firm's present office, at 756 Norton Avenue, was built and occupied in 1975.

Clyde Hendrick Realtors offers its clients consultation in investment and location of available residential, commercial, property management, insurance, and industrial properties. Robert Hendrick opened, and still manages, the Grand Haven office. Jett, who joined the company in 1957, manages the Muskegon office. In 1985 employment totaled thirty persons in sales and ten office personnel.

In 1978 Clyde Hendrick, one of the original founders of the Muskegon County Board of Realtors, was named Realtor Emeritus by the national association. Also in 1978 Norton Shores honored him as a Bicentennial Citizen, citing his fifty-six years of promoting his community. Hendrick kept an active hand in the business until three months before his death in 1981 at the age of eighty-eight.

Both Robert Hendrick and Gerald Jett have served as presidents and have been active on the North Ottawa and Muskegon Realtor boards. In addition, Robert was named Grand Haven Businessman of the Year in 1977.

Gerald Jett manages the Muskegon office.

Robert Hendrick, son of the founder, opened and still manages the Grand Haven office.

REID TOOL SUPPLY COMPANY

As an employee of a tool and die shop, Liberty G. Reid saw the task of obtaining tool room supplies as too costly and time consuming. He believed a solution would be to stock a warehouse with standard items and ship them promptly on customer demand.

Reid and his wife, Gloria, began working on his idea in the basement of their home on Baker Street in Muskegon Heights in 1948. In the thirty-eight years since then, Reid Tool Supply Company has matured into a flourishing business owned and operated by a second generation of Reids.

Paul A. Reid, company president since 1974, remembers carrying in packages from trucks and stuffing catalogs into envelopes as a child. His father devoted time away from his regular job to the business. His mother handled paperwork, scheduled shipments, and delivered orders to local customers.

The business soon outgrew the Reid home and was moved to a forty-by forty-foot office-warehouse, which was built at 250 Delano Avenue in 1952. Twelve years later Reid Tool constructed and moved into a large facility at 2233 Temple Street. Two additions expanded floor space to

28,000 square feet. The firm moved again in 1981 to its present plant at 2265 Black Creek Road. The Port City Industrial Park facility, designed for maximum employee efficiency and customer service, contains 50,000 square feet of floor space.

In the early days the Reids sent a sixteen-page catalog to 5,000 Midwest machine shops. The 1985 edition consisted of 202 pages and was shipped to 150,000 customers ranging from multinational corporations to one- and two-man shops. Twice a year the catalog is mailed to firms in the United States, Canada, Mexico, and other foreign countries.

Harold Schalk joined the company

Reid Tool Supply Company occupied this Port City Industrial Park facility, at 2265 Black Creek Road, in 1981.

in 1954 to develop a local industrial supply operation. After much success, he retired in 1975. Reid Tool opened a Grand Rapids branch office in 1984 to further extend its industrial supply business. Tooling Components, a Reid-related company in Muskegon Heights, manufactures part of the product line. Employment numbered eighty-eight persons at the three locations in 1985.

Liberty Reid saw his business prosper beyond his early expectations. Following Liberty's death in 1968, Mrs. Reid ran the company until 1974 when she retired and turned the management of the firm over to her son, Paul, who became president and board chairman.

Paul Reid heads up overall company operations. Bob Hommes currently is in charge of catalog sales, and Mike Strach is in charge of local sales. Product lines range from specialized tooling components and machine tool accessories to a full line of industrial supplies.

Paul's three sisters and two of their husbands have worked on Reid Tool Supply Company's management team. Janet Reid retired in 1985 after several years as purchasing agent. Ethel Strach works in accounting; Michael Strach is vice-president for local sales. Kay Bernard supervises incoming mail; John Bernard is vice-president in charge of telephone sales.

Paul Reid (right) heads up overall company operations while Bob Hommes (left) is in charge of catalog sales and Mike Strach (standing) manages local sales.

FLEET ENGINEERS, INC.

Back in the 1960s Louis E. Eklund, Jr., started to visualize some ideas to improve replacement and repair parts for over-the-road trucks. He began shaping his ideas into metal in a one-stall garage in Muskegon Heights and incorporated the business in 1965. Two decades later his brainchild, Fleet Engineers, Inc., was turning out truck parts in a modern factory and supplying them to truck manufacturers and repair shops through a world-wide network of 8,000 distributors.

On the way to success Eklund's business survived a disastrous fire and labor union strike. He credits his wife, Ann, with helping to get the company through the early years. He doesn't say so, but it is obvious that his own determination pushed the firm through and over obstacles in the path of progress.

Eklund had been working as purchasing director at West Michigan Steel Foundry, predecessor of Westran Corporation, when he decided to go on his own. He began work in a small garage off Sherman Boulevard between Sixth and Eighth streets in Muskegon Heights. Mrs. Eklund supported the family for the first three

Louis E. Eklund, Jr., founder.

years working as a registered nurse. They sold their house and second car to obtain working capital.

After a year in the little garage, Eklund rented a three-stall garage at the former Mona Lake Ice Company plant at Sixth and Sherman. He

Lou Eklund, Jr., began making truck parts in this one-stall garage off Sherman Boulevard in Muskegon Heights in 1963.

manufactured parts at that location for two and a half years.

Production began to outgrow the space, and Eklund saw the need to do his own finishing of metal parts. In 1967 he acquired Browning Manufacturing Company, a metal-finishing business on Hovey Avenue. He also purchased the General Building Materials warehouse at Sixth and Sherman, renovated the building, and consolidated all operations there in 1968.

Fire destroyed the factory in April 1970. Firefighters were able to wet down the separate office building and keep it from igniting. Eklund, who had been vacationing in Florida, returned home and set about to recoup his loss.

He sent copies of newspaper accounts and pictures of the fire along with notices to customers saying that Fleet Engineers was still in business. In addition, he contracted with other firms to manufacture parts and shipped them from the Hovey Avenue building he had retained.

Insurance covered only part of the fire loss. INDEX, an agency established by the Muskegon Area Chamber of Commerce to promote industrial development, provided a $5,000 grant from its Park Fund. Eklund's firm bought land in the Port City Industrial Park, south of East Laketon Avenue, and construction began on a new factory and office building.

Fleet Engineers moved in and resumed production six months after the fire. In 1985 the fifth plant expansion was begun. It would give the firm 95,000 square feet of work space.

When Eklund began his business he had one employee, a semiretired man who worked in the office twenty hours a week. Today Fleet Engineers has seventy-five employees who manufacture, stock, and distribute products nationwide from five warehouses.

The company produces twenty

Fleet Engineers' offices and plant at 1800 East Keating Avenue present a trim appearance in the Port City Industrial Park.

families of truck and trailer parts, each with many variations. Individual products number several hundred. Brackets to hold mud flaps and fenders are the firm's major products. Workers also fabricate such components as doors, hinges, and support structures.

Fleet Engineers produces body components and accessories for heavy-duty highway truck manufacturers and repair companies. Customers include privately owned firms and the U.S. Department of Defense. The company's parts also go into over-the-road tractors, semi- and full trailers, and military vehicles such as the HUMVEE, which replaced the familiar Army jeep.

One of the highlights of Eklund's career is that he pioneered the hiring of retired persons in the Muskegon area. At one time in the 1970s Fleet

Engineers employed as many as thirty part-time senior workers. "They were former company presidents, chemists, engineers, plant managers, who could not cope with retirement," Eklund says. "I was gifted with a lot of talented and dedicated people."

However, the retiree work force was cut in half as the result of a dispute over labor union representation. Some of the part-time employees' homes were damaged and vandalized and, as a result, they quit working.

Fleet Engineers also hires Muskegon High School and Muskegon Community College students on a part-time basis through the schools' work-study programs. "My wife made it possible for me to get started," Eklund says. "And I have been fortunate to have this reservoir of talent to work for me for a number of years."

In addition to operating Fleet Engineers, Inc., Eklund has worked to improve the climate for business and industry in Muskegon and Michigan.

He is a director of the Muskegon Manufacturers' and Employers' Association and has worked extensively on the chamber of commerce's workers' compensation reform, as well as on legislative and political action committees.

Truck-trailer parts and accessories made by Fleet Engineers include door hardware, landing gear, cranked gear support, and tarpaulin bows.

CLOCK FUNERAL HOME

Four generations of the Clock family have met a basic community need in providing funeral service for Muskegon County families.

Tiede Clock began in 1897 what was to become a tradition. Two of his grandsons and two great-grandsons continue it today, operating funeral homes in Muskegon and Whitehall.

At age twenty-three Tiede Clock operated a store on Jefferson Street across from the Muskegon City Hall. He sold paint, wallpaper, and artists' supplies.

One spring day in 1897 his uncle, Del Clark, a police officer, walked into the store and asked Clock if he would be interested in becoming an undertaker. In that era surviving family members usually had a carpenter or cabinetmaker build a coffin in which to bury their dead. Clock decided he could provide such services while continuing to meet the needs of artists and home decorators. He began his undertaking business with enthusiasm, $125 in cash, and support from his relatives.

Undertaking was a sideline to the art and paint supply store until Tiede became a full-time funeral director in 1900. T. Clock & Co., Undertakers and Funeral Furnishers, grew and relocated three times in the next twenty years. It was moved from Jefferson Street to Pine Street and to two different buildings off Western Avenue near the downtown business district.

The name was changed to Clock Funeral Home in 1920, and a building designed specifically for funeral service was erected at the corner of Sanford Street and Grand Avenue, its present location.

Tiede Clock was elected county coroner and held that office for twenty-one years. It was the coroner's duty to establish the cause of death in cases of violent, accidental, or questionable deaths. Coroner Clock convened many a coroner's jury in those twenty-one years.

A need for more space brought about remodeling of the funeral home at Sanford Street and Grand Avenue in 1928. The garage was converted into a chapel, a new garage

was built, and an office area was erected apart from the other facilities.

Clock's two sons, Theodore G. "Ted" and Thomas C., assisted in the business after they graduated from Worsham School of Embalming in Chicago.

The company's services first expanded outside the city in 1939, when Tiede's son-in-law, Darrell Nollar, opened a branch in Ravenna. However, wartime economies forced the closing of the branch in 1944, and Nollar rejoined the Muskegon firm. Thomas' brother-in-law, Richard Pattenger (who died in 1981), was also associated with the company.

Tiede Clock retired from the business in 1944, and Thomas Clock, Sr., took over management of the firm. Tragedy struck when a Muskegon Lake boating accident took the life of Ted Clock in 1945. The Clocks marked their fiftieth year in business with another remodeling of the funeral home in 1947.

The third generation of the Clock family entered the business in 1952,

Tiede Clock

Thomas C. Clock, Sr.

Theodore G. Clock

Clock Funeral Home, in Muskegon, after the 1960 remodeling was completed.

when Thomas C. Clock, Jr., and Wayne A. Clock graduated from Wayne State University's College of Mortuary Science in Detroit. Four years later Jack Clock completed the third-generation echelon, joining his father and brothers after graduation from Wayne State. Jack died in 1966 after a long illness.

Growth prompted further expansion, and a new chapel with permanent church-type pew seating was built in 1960. It included a secluded family room and a special enclosure for the old pipe organ, the pride and joy of founder Tiede Clock who had it built in Milwaukee, Wisconsin, especially for his funeral home. A corporation was formed in 1962.

Over the years the Clocks purchased and razed nearby houses to provide space for parking. In addition, offices were moved near the chapel and the Grand Avenue entrance was closed.

Growth extended to the White Lake area in 1971, when the Clocks purchased the Purdy Funeral Home. Tom Clock, Jr., moved his family to Whitehall to manage this branch, while Wayne remained in Muskegon as its manager. The firm also acquired the Gee Funeral Home on Colby Street in Whitehall in 1972. All White Lake area services were then consolidated at the facility at 413 South Mears Avenue. The Whitehall home was expanded and improved in 1972 with the construction of a large chapel, family room, offices, and other facilities.

Thomas Clock, Sr., who had gone into semiretirement in 1971, died in 1981 at the age of seventy-six. He had lived to see the fourth generation of his family enter the business. Thomas Clock III joined the firm in 1980 after graduation from Indiana College of Mortuary Science. And in 1986 Dale R. Clock joined his father, Wayne, in operating the Muskegon home upon graduation from Worsham.

In addition to providing funeral services, the Clock family has continued the tradition of community service established by Tiede Clock. Thomas Sr. was a longtime Lions Club member and was also active in the Berean Church. Thomas Jr. has served on the Muskegon Community College board since 1963 and was elected chairman by fellow trustees in 1985. He has also been active in Trinity Lutheran Church in Muskegon and Faith Lutheran Church in Whitehall, as well as the Muskegon Optimist and Whitehall Rotary clubs. Wayne, past trustee and chairman of the Muskegon Board of Education, has also served Samuel Lutheran Church in Muskegon and has been an active Rotarian.

In 1986 Clock Funeral Home's licensed staff consisted of four Clocks: Thomas Jr., Thomas III, Wayne, and Dale, along with Garth Wiswell, Donald Stidham, Kenneth Gowell, Bradley King, and Darrell Nollar.

Thomas C. Clock, Jr.

Wayne A. Clock

159

SEALED POWER CORPORATION

An automotive industry giant was born December 10, 1911, when two Muskegon men pooled their savings to begin manufacturing engine piston rings using a new method.

Charles E. Johnson, an expert in things mechanical, and Paul R. Beardsley, skilled in sales and finance, obtained some castings and machines and began working evenings and weekends in a small rented warehouse at Terrace and Market streets. Their Piston Ring Company was renamed Sealed Power Corporation in 1931. By 1985 the firm had become the largest Muskegon-based corporation in sales volume, with manufacturing and marketing facilities spread nationwide and throughout the Free World.

In the early 1900s Johnson learned of a new method of producing piston rings. There are two kinds of piston rings: One seals gases in the combustion chamber above the moving piston, and the second maintains an even oil film on the cylinder wall. The new method involved individual casting instead of cutting rings off an iron cylinder.

The partners had no customers for their product until Beardsley took an armload of rings and walked across the street to the Continental Motors Corporation plant. He convinced Continental to try the rings in some of its engines. The rings worked so well that Continental placed a sizable order. Other engine manufacturers soon followed suit.

A year after its founding Piston Ring Company moved to a one-story building on Sanford Street. A foundry was constructed in 1913 and later was doubled in size. In addition, a four-story machine shop was erected to meet pre-World War I production needs.

The Sanford Street plant has remained Sealed Power's primary facility for casting and finishing piston rings and includes the Corporate Research and Development Center. Corporate and administrative staffs moved into the new Terrace Plaza seven-floor complex in 1978.

Sealed Power has three other plants in Muskegon. The Harvey Street plant, built in 1962 and expanded twice, produces cylinder sleeves and diesel engine rings. The Hy-Lift Division plant on Keating Avenue (the former Johnson Products plant, acquired by Sealed Power in 1972) manufactures engine valve tappets. The Fluid Control Division on East Sherman Boulevard was established in 1984 to design and produce a new line of electrohydraulic valves.

Charles E. Johnson's son, Paul, led the corporation in the 1950s and 1960s. The co-founder's grandson, Charles E. Johnson II, became president of the firm in 1985. At that time Robert D. Tuttle became chairman of the board, replacing Edward I. Schalon, who had been chairman for several years.

Over the years Sealed Power Corporation has acquired several other companies in order to improve and broaden its product lines and manufacturing capabilities. Most recent acquisitions added manufacturing and distributing of specialized maintenance tools and equipment, hydraulic products, and window and door hardware.

Sealed Power Corporation's world headquarters in the Terrace Plaza, Muskegon. Excavators for the building turned up remnants of the warehouse where the company was started in 1911.

PRO-PHONE COMMUNICATIONS, INC.

First it was a telephone answering service. Now it is a computerized electronic communications center serving business, industry, professional people, and households.

Ellen A. Ford and her husband, Jack, have been building their service companies' customer lists since Ellen started work with Professional Phone Answering. Their other two related firms are Pro-Phone Communications, Inc., and Business Communications Center, Inc. All three operate from 2340 Glade Street in Muskegon Heights.

The business got its start in 1953 when George Abbott, a General Telephone Company employee, set up a telephone answering service at Jefferson Street and Webster Avenue. George and Louise Young bought the operation, named it Professional Phone Answering Service, and moved it to the Arcade Building at Jefferson and Clay avenues in the 1960s. At that time the service was operated only during daytime business hours.

When the Youngs, Ellen Ford's aunt and uncle, could no longer run the operation, Ellen was called in to do some office work. In 1971 she and her husband purchased the business and moved it to 95 Webster Avenue.

Electing to promote and expand the service, Ellen installed modern switching equipment. Secretarial service was established in 1973. Pro-Phone Communications, Inc., was formed two years later to fulfill the demand for direct-dial paging and mobile telephone service. Business Communications Center, Inc., was organized in 1981 to offer various services to business people. That same year Jack Ford joined Ellen to help operate the enterprises.

In order to acquire enough space for equipment and the operators, the Fords built the Glade Street structure and moved operations there in 1983. Twenty full- and part-time employees

operate the center 24 hours a day, 365 days a year.

Customers of the center include large and small businesses; dentists, physicians, and business people, ranging from company presidents to janitors; manufacturing sales representatives; and firms without staffed offices. The area served covers Muskegon, Ottawa, Oceana, and Mason counties and stretches east to Newaygo County and covers all Grand Rapids.

All incoming phone calls go through a master computer monitor that routes them to a "live" telephone secretary. The computer records each call and tabulates the number of calls per hour so the manager will know how many telephone secretaries are needed to handle peak volume.

Ellen Ford became the first woman

Pro-Phone Communications, Inc., a computerized electronic communications center, operates from 2340 Glade Street in Muskegon Heights.

to head the Muskegon Area Chamber of Commerce in 1985 and is a past president of that organization's Women's Division. She currently serves as president of the Michigan Association of Radio Systems and is a past president of the Michigan Telephone Answering Association. In 1983 Ellen received Quadrangle's Businesswoman of the Year Award and in 1985 she received the Zonta Club's Woman of Achievement Award.

Pro-Phone telephone secretaries answer twenty-four hours a day.

THE SHAW-WALKER COMPANY

The Shaw-Walker Company story could best be summed up as the right man and his colleagues doing the right thing in the right place at the right time.

The man was Louis Carlisle "L.C." Walker. The thing he and his contemporaries and successors did was design and manufacture top-quality office furniture and equipment to fit the needs of business, sometimes before the executives recognized their needs.

The place, of course, is Muskegon. The time, one year before the century turned, was right for two reasons: Muskegon was hearing the death rattle of its fabled lumber industry, while business was approaching the brink of mushrooming growth into multilocation offices with the resulting need for close work station communication and the systematic filing of ever-burgeoning business records. This fortuitous concourse of circumstances made Shaw-Walker the nation's foremost manufacturer devoted solely to the production of office furniture and record-keeping systems.

Throughout the twentieth century Muskegon has benefited from Shaw-

Shaw Walker

Walker's payroll and corporate taxes plus its unbridled community service and direct financial contributions to the city's business, education, cultural, and recreational institutions.

L.C. Walker and Arch W. Shaw were two young men working as clerks in the Fred Macey office furnishings mail-order house in Grand Rapids, Michigan. Convinced they could do better with their own business, but not wishing to compete directly with their employer, the pair moved forty-five miles northwest to Muskegon. On March 9, 1899, they filed articles of incorporation for The Shaw-Walker Company at the Muskegon County Courthouse.

To manufacture their first product—a nine-inch oak box with three-by five-inch file cards and alphabetical tab indexes—they obtained a bank loan of $100 and bought five pieces of equipment: a cutting machine, two foot-powered tabbing machines, and two printing presses. The partners began work in two small storerooms in the old Muskegon Opera House. They advertised in local

periodicals that the $1.95 file boxes would serve as "complete office systems" designed to alleviate the clutter of paper that sometimes covered the harried executive's rolltop, pigeonhole desk.

The index file business grew so rapidly that the factory soon was moved to a small building near the Railway Express office on Western Avenue. But that structure proved insufficient almost before it was occupied. As a result, the first factory building was erected in 1903 at the firm's present site, Western at Division Street. Over the years office and factory buildings totaling one million square feet of floor space have been added to fill the 25-acre site.

Systems has always been the key word for Shaw-Walker. The company went on to develop systems to simplify and streamline office work procedures that had kept clerks and secretaries bogged down in tiresome, repetitive manual labor.

The first product of The Shaw-Walker Company was this oak box filled with index-tabbed file cards.

L.C. Walker

Heated by a potbellied stove, Shaw-Walker workers turned out wooden filing boxes and tabbed index cards in this factory on Western Avenue near the Railway Express office. The photo was taken in 1901.

Shaw-Walker continuously updated and redesigned its products to meet the changing needs of business. L.C. Walker believed the standard office desk height of 30.5 inches was too high for efficient and comfortable use by the average office worker. He pioneered a 29-inch desk design that the industry soon came to accept as standard.

Long before the advent of calculators and computers, Walker and his staff of experts worked out a simplified method of figuring company payrolls. Their system eliminated 60 percent of the time required to calculate withholding taxes, Social Security, union dues, hospitalization, and other paycheck deductions, and em-

To keep its customers informed as to the use of the file card boxes and other products, Shaw-Walker printed and distributed a booklet entitled *Systems.* That booklet is generally regarded as the first house organ published by a manufacturer in the United States.

Systems readily captured the attention of business people. In 1902 Shaw left the young company and took the publication with him to Chicago. There he published it under the title *Magazine of Business.* Shaw's publishing house prospered. After a merger with McGraw-Hill, the magazine was titled *Business Week* and is still widely read in the world of commerce.

Walker continued as chief executive officer of The Shaw-Walker Company, which expanded its product line to include multidrawer filing cabinets, desks, and chairs, made of steel and designed for efficient, long-term use.

Walker was a firm believer in keeping his salesmen and present and potential customers informed of innovations in office management. In 1924 Shaw-Walker's sales department began to publish another magazine called *The Skyscraper.* Its name came from the company emblem, which shows a man jumping into an opened bottom drawer of a filing cabinet accompanied by the words, "Built Like a Skyscraper." This became one of the best known trademarks in the country and has been revived by the firm in recent years.

The steel framework of a Shaw-Walker filing cabinet compares with New York City's Woolworth Building under construction in the early 1900s. The comparison resulted in the company's emblem with the inscription, "Built Like a Skyscraper."

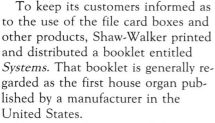

President Dwight D. Eisenhower leans on a Shaw-Walker filing cabinet while talking to his friend and speech writer, Kevin McCann, on Ike's last day in the White House in 1961.

An aerial view of The Shaw-Walker Company plant at Western Avenue and Division Street.

ployers throughout the nation soon adopted it.

An 1896 graduate of the University of Michigan with a bachelor's of science degree, Walker was well informed in the area of business management, especially office functions. He went on to author two books and several articles on the subject.

His first book, *The Office and Tomorrow's Business,* was published in 1930 and was still in print two decades later. In the book Walker stated that business executives were too inclined to merely tolerate an office as an expense necessary to continue in business. He suggested that they view the office as the brains and nerve center of their company. Offices, he wrote, should be well thought out and planned in advance with efficient layout, furniture, equipment, and equally effective personnel to create and file all the records necessary to carry on operations.

His second volume, entitled *Distributed Leisure,* came out a year later. In it Walker expressed the somewhat startling premise that industry produces leisure time for employees on a co-equal basis with the company's product or service. Hence, executives should help provide means so that employees have ample facilities to enjoy their leisure time. He described leisure as "unemployment with the fear taken out."

Unemployment was a hard fact of life for millions of workers in the depressed 1930s. Walker proposed to alleviate it with a Share-The-Work program. He already had put this program into effect at his own firm during the 1921 recession and again when the Great Depression began in 1930.

In an article published in the 1933 *Annals of the American Academy,* Walker wrote: "The hope of the movement is to spread the available work, not only in industrial plants but also in offices, stores, banks, and other service institutions and community administration activities. It is not contemplated that any employer should reduce the time and earnings of a worker who has not a margin beyond his actual needs."

The idea was promoted widely by the National Association of Manufacturers, of which Walker was vice-president. However, it was never adopted by President Franklin Roosevelt's new administration.

L.C. Walker was an astute businessman as well as industrialist. He served as director and president of Hackley Union National Bank for twenty-eight years. In 1933 he helped organize Muskegon Federal Savings and Loan Association and was elected its first president. Among his many civic and fraternal activities, Walker served nine years on the Muskegon Board of Education and promoted the college campus-type construction of the senior high school.

Walker, a firm believer in recreation, also organized the Muskegon Progress and Development Fund, which obtained two million dollars to establish seven playfields throughout the community and nearly two million dollars more to build the downtown sports arena that bears his name. Eight years before the arena was opened in 1960, he had conceived it as a "playground under roof where boys and girls can play during our long winter months." Young people of the community staged a Salute to L.C. Walker when the arena was dedicated on October 27, 1960.

Walker maintained an active role in his company through his late seventies, devoting his attention to research and engineering. Muskegon and a widespread business community mourned his death on October 5, 1963, at the age of eighty-eight.

His son, Shaw Walker, had joined the firm in 1938 and was named executive vice-president in 1952. He became president of the firm six years later. Following his father's death, Shaw became president and treasurer of the L.C. and Margaret Walker Foundation and retained those offices after he retired from the company in 1982.

The foundation supports the arts and educational institutions in Muskegon and other cities. The Walker Gallery in the Muskegon Museum of Art was opened in 1983 and houses a collection of fine art prints. The foundation also financed the construction of the Walker Memorial Library, the North Muskegon Community Center adjoining the library, and Walker Park on the bluff overlooking Muskegon Lake.

John S.W. Spofford, one of L.C. Walker's grandsons, became president of The Shaw-Walker Company in 1980 and two years later was elected chief executive officer of the family-owned corporation. Spofford entered the business as manager of international sales in the New York City office after ten years in international banking.

By the mid-1980s Shaw-Walker management was recognizing the service of third-generation employees.

Of the 780 then on the payroll, 230 had worked for the firm for twenty-five or more years.

From the small rooms where Shaw and Walker began their business, The Shaw-Walker Company has grown into a nationwide organization. The Muskegon plant houses corporate headquarters and the Furniture Systems Division. Shaw-Walker also manufactures business forms through its subsidiary, Master-Craft Corp., located in Kalamazoo, Michigan; Valdosta, Georgia; and Norman, Oklahoma.

In the early 1970s Shaw-Walker introduced panel systems for open office use. A line of computer support furniture followed later. In 1985 the company introduced a new line of wooden desks, primarily designed for executives, bringing the preferred material for office furniture full circle back to wood from steel.

Today The Shaw-Walker Company's products are distributed through 600 dealerships and the firm's wholesale system of regional

John S.W. Spofford

branches. Product showrooms are maintained in Chicago, New York City, San Francisco, Los Angeles, and Washington, D.C.

An office systems layout with computer support furniture designed and built by Shaw-Walker for a high-technology office.

MUSKEGON GLASS COMPANY, INC.

James J. McDermott (second from right) founded Muskegon Glass Company in 1908. Photo circa 1912

For nearly eight decades the McDermott family has sold and installed the portals that admit sunlight into the homes and business places of Muskegon.

James Joseph McDermott founded his business in 1908 under the name it bears today, Muskegon Glass Company, Inc. His son, Harvey Francis McDermott, ran the firm for twenty-six years; his daughter-in-law, Grace, operated it for fifteen years following the death of her husband, Harvey. William J. McDermott, the third generation of his family to be involved in the business, has been operating president since his mother retired in 1982.

Founder James McDermott was a twelve-year-old orphan when he migrated from Ireland to Chicago to live with relatives. He moved to Grand Rapids, Michigan, where he met and married a young woman named Pearl Marie Stevenson. Soon

thereafter, the couple moved to Muskegon.

McDermott was nineteen years old when he opened his glass shop on First Street near Clay Avenue on the present site of the Hardy-Herpolsheimer Store's furniture section. His first specialty item was stained glass, which was in demand for some of the more opulent Muskegon homes as well as the city's churches. In 1938 McDermott bought an old hotel building on the northeast corner of Pine and Clay, removed the second floor, and moved his glass business into the ground floor.

Harvey McDermott, who had worked in the business as a young man, took over Muskegon Glass in 1941 upon the death of his father. In 1966 the shop was moved to the Panyard building on Concord Street.

The following year Harvey passed away. His wife, Grace, who had kept the company's books for fifteen years, assumed control of the business and operated it by herself until she retired in 1982 and moved to Florida. Her son, William J. McDermott, who had

worked in all phases of the glass business for ten years, then became company president. His wife, Denise, and a sister, Mrs. Jane Mills, currently do the bookkeeping and office work.

William McDermott says the firm values highly the services of two veteran employees—Willy Forester and Mart Johnson—both of whom have worked for Muskegon Glass for forty years. Forester's son, Bill, is a twenty-year employee.

In 1978 McDermott built and moved into a shop at 777 Pine Street next door to the old former hotel building where his grandfather and father had served the glass needs of Muskegonites. He was forced to have the old building razed in 1982 after water gushing from a broken street main undermined the structure.

In addition to residential glazing in the form of single-pane glass, sealed double-pane picture windows, and shatterproof plastic, Muskegon Glass Company, Inc., also installs custom-size mirrors and tabletops. Commercial installations include storefronts and new buildings of all types.

Grace and Harvey McDermott in front of the firm's 42 Concord location.

APEX WELDING GASES AND SUPPLIES, INC.

Apex Welding Gases and Supplies, Inc., has kept pace with the growing welding industry for more than fifty years. A leading western Michigan industrial gas and welding supply distributor, the firm has had two owners since it was founded in 1932.

Earl Tupes formed the business after losing his job during the Depression. Kent I. VandeVrede has operated the firm since he purchased it in 1970.

Tupes was employed by Michigan Oxy-Hydric Company on Western Avenue when the Linde Division of Union Carbide took it over. He became a salesman for Linde, but the extreme business slump terminated this position. He founded Tupes Spring and Welding Service on Peck Street at Holbrook in 1932, moving to the rear of 2028 Peck Street and later to a former grocery store at 2034 Peck.

In 1936 Tupes expanded by opening a branch store in Saginaw and sold welding supplies and equipment from his truck to shops across the lower peninsula between the two cities. His son, Robert, took over the Saginaw store in 1947.

Apex Welding Gases and Supplies

Peck Street in 1961. Tupes Spring and Welding Service, forerunner of Apex Welding Gases and Supplies, Inc., was orginally located behind 2028 Peck Street.

was incorporated in 1940 with Abbie Tupes as president. She signed all business papers with the initials A.R. to disguise the fact that she was a businesswoman. Tupes Spring and Welding Service was incorporated in 1962 with Earl Tupes as president.

Kent VandeVrede had worked in welding supply stores in Lansing with his father and on his own in Adrian. After learning that the Muskegon businesses were for sale, he came to town in 1970 and worked for the firm while the purchase agreements were being written. In March of that year, with purchase completed, he merged the two corporations under the Apex name. Tupes stayed with the firm for a year to help the new owner get started and then retired; he passed away in 1985. Mrs. Tupes eventually moved to California.

In April 1970 fire gutted the Bishop Motor Express Company building next door to the Apex facility. VandeVrede purchased the Bishop property and erected a new building. In 1974 he acquired the Fisher property to the south and consolidated the operations under one roof in the present building. In 1971 Apex installed its first customer liquid oxygen system in Holland, and nine years later the firm opened a Holland branch.

In 1985 Apex had seventeen people on its payroll. Senior employees were Philip Young, office manager, forty-six years with the firm; Harold Swanson, repair and service manager, forty years; and Bob Hansen, truck route driver and oxygen pumper, thirty-four years.

VandeVrede says that Apex Welding Gases and Supplies, Inc., has grown from a general store type of business by keeping abreast of the many advances in welding and cutting technology. Some of these advances include computerized welding and cutting machines, robotic welding systems, and the company's continued expansion in the bulk liquid gas distribution market.

Today Apex Welding Gases and Supplies, Inc., at 2044 Peck Street, has expanded over much of the block where it began in 1932.

LIFT TECH INTERNATIONAL, INC.
CRANE AND HOIST OPERATIONS

Industrial cranes and hoists have been built continuously in a plant on West Broadway Avenue in Muskegon Heights since the Gay Nineties. Since that time the business has undergone several changes in name, ownership, and management, and at times has manufactured products other than lifting devices. As recently as April 1, 1986, Lift Tech International, Inc., Crane and Hoist Operations, began business with local management dedicated to continuing the manufacture of the fine hoisting machinery that the company has become famous for. The new management is willing to pursue the investment necessary to reestablish the reputation for innovation that the business was founded upon.

The business, which began as the Shaw Electric Crane Co., founded by Alton J. Shaw, was moved to Muskegon from Milwaukee, Wisconsin, in 1890. Shaw had been a draftsman/master mechanic at the Edwin P.

Alton J. Shaw, founder of the Shaw Electric Crane Works in Muskegon, predecessor of the Crane and Hoist Operations of Lift Tech International, Inc.

Allis Co. foundry in Milwaukee, when a lift system known as a "flying rope" crane collapsed under a ten-ton load, killing the operator. That tragedy prompted Shaw to design a safer and more efficient crane.

Shaw's principle was that each prime component of a crane—hoist, trolley, and bridge—should be powered by its own reversible electric motor. The crane that killed the worker at the Allis foundry was one of the standard-type lifters of the era powered by a single stationary steam engine with power transmitted through a system of ropes. The three primary components were activated by individual clutch systems. The cranes were difficult to operate and malfunctioned frequently.

With approval from his employers, Shaw designed and built a crane driven by three electric motors. Believed to be the first such machine in the country and probably the world, it proved to be so much more efficient and safer than existing cranes that visiting heavy-industry executives asked to have one built for their factories.

Shaw received early encouragement in his crane-building project from a friend, John G. Emery, Jr. The pair went on to form a partnership and built thirty of the new electric cranes in two years, working in a Milwaukee machine shop.

On the other side of Lake Michigan, Muskegon civic leaders were ever on watch for new businesses to replace the lumber industry that had consumed its timber supply. Contact was made, and the Muskegonites convinced Shaw and Emery to move their new industry to Muskegon and helped the partners obtain a building site on Broadway Avenue.

Production began at the Shaw Electric Crane Works in 1891. The factory has been expanded several times, but the cornerstone of the original building is still in place at

John G. Emery, Jr., joined the firm as partner and remained actively involved until 1942.

the Park Street gate. Shaw was president of the firm when it moved to Michigan. Emery maintained an active role on the Shaw-Box advisory board until 1942. He also served as an official of Lumberman's Bank.

Shaw and Emery sold their cranes exclusively through Manning, Maxwell & Moore, Inc., of Stratford, Connecticut. In 1905 that firm purchased Shaw Electric Crane Works and four other manufacturing companies whose products it had marketed. The Shaw Electric Crane Division built heavy-duty cranes for industry. In 1931 Manning, Maxwell & Moore bought out Box Crane & Hoist Corp., which had manufactured cranes and hoists in Philadelphia. The merged firms then became Manning, Maxwell & Moore's Shaw-Box Crane and Hoist Division.

Shaw-Box continued to manufacture the Load Lifter heavy-duty crane developed by Box and the lower-capacity Load Lifter Junior engineered by Shaw. Popularity of the

Lift Tech International's Crane and Hoist Operations plant, still on West Broadway Avenue, has about nineteen acres under roof. The smokestack and dark roof area (left of center) marks the original factory, built in 1890.

lighter units led to the production of the Budgit electric hoist and a line of related products that followed. Success of the Budgit line led management to try a new marketing concept. The light-load hoists were shipped to dealers for direct sale to customers; previously, the hoists had been produced on order.

Additional products manufactured at the Broadway Avenue plant have included shallow well and post hole drilling rigs, butterfly valves and mud pumps, and other equipment for oil drillers. Small radio and television re-

The Shaw Electric Crane Works' original factory was built in 1890 on West Broadway Avenue at Park Street in Muskegon Heights.

lay towers also were produced. In recent years, however, production has been limited to Shaw-Box industrial cranes, wire rope electric- and air- powered hoists, Budgit air and electric hoists, kits for assembling cranes, and Tugit lever-operated chain hoists.

BENNETT PUMP COMPANY

Thomas B. "Bert" Bennett.

The Bennett Pump Company story goes back to 1920, when Thomas B. "Bert" Bennett operated Muskegon's first drive-in service station and taxi service at his garage at Clay Avenue and Second Street. In the sixty-five years since then, the firm has developed into a leading manufacturer of petroleum product dispensers and claims to have installed one of every five new pumps along the world's highways.

As Bennett hand packed car transmissions with grease, he began looking for better ways to transfer lubricants from container to automobile. His search led him to A.J. Woods of Grand Rapids, who had developed a bucket with a foot-operated pump but lacked the capital to fill a backlog of orders for his grease dispenser.

Bennett purchased Woods' business in 1920. He improved the design, rented a shop at Terrace and Market streets, and started to manu-

facture pump buckets under the name Bennett Injector Company.

Woods' bucket was soon replaced with a device Bennett designed to pump grease from wooden barrels. When refiners switched to shipping grease in steel drums, Bennett developed his first hand-crank pump to fit them. He also came out with a lever-operated oil pump and a 25-pound grease bucket with a hand pump attached.

L.A. "Roy" Prescott, who taught drawing at Muskegon High School, began working for the firm on a part-time basis in 1922. Years later, as company manager, he recalled for salesmen the firm's modest beginnings. He said that often Bennett would design pump parts on wrapping paper from a nearby meat market and carve master patterns for castings with a jackknife.

Business increased tenfold in the first three years. In 1924 Bennett moved the company to its present site on Wood Street at Broadway in Muskegon Heights after purchasing the small factory of a failed motor manufacturer and the block of land

around it for $24,000. A name change followed the move to larger quarters. The Bennett Injector Company became Bennett Pump Company, with the sales division being called Service Station Equipment Company.

Prescott became a full-time employee in 1925. One of his first assignments was to design a visible barrel-type oil pump operated by a hand crank. The pinion and crank were placed below the glass cylinder to avoid breaking the glass, an occurrence common in competitors' products. The first crank-operated oil pump failed to win widespread acceptance, but a revised model soon made the grade.

When he could not interest enough investors to finance an expansion in order to manufacture additional products, Bennett talked his stockholders into selling the company to Service Station Equipment Ltd. of Toronto, Canada, in 1928. The new owners provided capital for Bennett to begin producing gasoline pumps. The first electrically powered metering pumps were shipped from the plant in 1929, with visual-type gas pumps coming soon after.

The Canadian parent company then moved its Eco Tireflator (air compressor) manufacturing facilities from Bryan, Ohio, to Muskegon, giving Bennett Pump Company a more complete product line for the auto service industry. Business boomed, with sales peaking at $3 million in 1930.

However, the Great Depression soon began to take its toll on busi-

Bennett Pump Company offices and factory on Wood Street at Broadway Avenue, Muskegon Heights.

ness. Toronto management decided to consolidate U.S. manufacturing in a plant it had built in Conshohocken, Pennsylvania, to produce water heaters and the same type of service equipment made in Muskegon.

Bert Bennett could see no way out and resigned as president and general manager in 1930, at which time Prescott was appointed manager of the Muskegon plant. When the factory was locked up on March 6, 1933, Muskegon's unemployment rolls soared. Many workers believed their jobs were lost permanently.

Service Station Equipment Ltd. had merged with John Wood Company in 1932. However, combining water heater and pump production didn't work out, and in 1937 the factory was moved back to the Muskegon plant where the manufacturing areas were redesigned for more efficiency. Prescott was reinstated as general manager, and nearly half the original work force was rehired to assist in the move and resume production.

Unfortunately, Bennett did not live to see the company he had founded return home. He died in 1933 while trying to form a new corporation to keep the plant in Muskegon.

All pump manufacturing ceased for the duration of World War II. Converted to war production, the firm was the first in Muskegon to receive the Army-Navy "E" Award for excellence. In the late 1940s gasoline pumps accounted for half the company's output, and the firm became the largest U.S. producer of automatic tire-inflating equipment.

In 1950 the firm's name was changed again as it became the Bennett Pump Division of John Wood Company. That year Bennett Pump came out with something new—a combined air and water service unit to be placed next to gas pumps. The following year Prescott

The visible pump was produced from 1929 to 1940.

retired and was succeeded as general manager by Arch F. Jordan.

Bennett introduced several innovations in the 1950s. They included the first gasoline pumps with curved-glass dial faces, single and twin units capable of serving two cars at once, a fluorescent-lighted dial face, and the first electric pump for farm use. A swivel to prevent hose twisting was added in 1967.

Anthes Imperial Ltd. of Canada acquired John Wood Company in 1964. Four years later Molson Breweries merged with Anthes, establishing Molson Industries, Ltd., a multinational, multiproduct corporation. Phillip W. Keesen took over as president of Bennett Pump in 1966. He retired in 1973, at which time Peter M. Turner became president and chief operating officer.

In 1975, when the energy shortage and business recession set in, Bennett found it necessary to move its hand-pump operations from Hart to Muskegon.

Meanwhile, the firm responded to another challenge, the design and development of an electronic self-serve fueling system. With the use of microprocessor chips and programmable

memory, in October 1975 Bennett introduced the first computerized service station fueling system. With this success, more factory space was required, so the Eco Tireflator business was sold. To further maintain its quality status in the industry, Bennett opened its own electronic assemblies manufacturing plant in Grand Rapids in 1978.

Alfred C. Raschke became president of the firm in 1978, replacing Turner who resigned. Molson Industries sold Bennett Pump to an international group of investors headed by SATAM of France. Other associate firms are Schiedt & Bachmann of West Germany, Hockman Lewis, Ltd., of New Jersey, and Industrias Guillermo of Mexico.

In May 1981 Bennett opened a remanufacturing plant in Rock Hill, South Carolina. At this plant old pumps are remanufactured, and when they leave they look just like new.

At the time of the sale, Bennett Pump Company moved from subsidiary status to that of a free-standing corporation. John R. Mahone, formerly an executive with U.S., Swedish, and Canadian companies, became president of Bennett Pump in 1983.

Production of Bennett's multiproduct dispenser began in 1983.

BUEHRLE ENGINEERING COMPANY, INC.

Clarence J. Buehrle came to Muskegon with his family in 1919 because the teenager's mother had been advised to leave the Chicago area's polluted air. He went back to the Windy City for training as a tool and die maker, returned to Muskegon, worked in several local industries, and started his own business in 1940.

Buehrle Engineering Company, Inc., stands today at 856 East Broadway Avenue as a product of his work. The firm, which is owned and operated by a son and son-in-law of the founder, produces aluminum and zinc die castings for manufacturers in Muskegon and elsewhere.

When Buehrle returned to Chicago, he began to learn tool and die making at Western Electric Company. He attended night school and became involved in the research and development of early sound films and also repaired cars as a sideline.

Accompanied by his wife of one year, Alma Sandwick, Buehrle moved back to Muskegon in 1925. He

Donald G. Buehrle, president.

Clarence J. Buehrle, founder.

worked for Continental Motors Corporation, Brunswick Corporation, and at other tool and die shops in Muskegon, Grand Rapids, and Detroit. For three years he was a master mechanic at the Borg-Warner Norge Division plant in Muskegon Heights.

Buehrle organized his business in 1940, starting work in a machine shop at 22 East Webster Avenue. He began with one man and had six men by the end of the year making tools, dies, and fixtures for manufacturers of refrigerators, washing machines, and stoves.

In 1941 the company moved into a portion of the Clark Floor Sanding Machine building at 30 Clay Avenue, and began manufacturing the first wartime products—landing struts for Army gliders. At that time employment numbered sixty persons. Buehrle was also responsible for managing production levels at six other Michigan tool and die firms. General Dwight D. Eisenhower later sent Buehrle a citation for his war production efforts.

In 1944 Buehrle constructed a new

plant at the East Broadway address. He also designed and built a zinc die casting machine and later added aluminum casting equipment. Four additions brought the plant to 17,000 square feet by 1974.

In 1985 Buehrle Engineering employed seventeen persons, with 90 percent of the production going to local manufacturers. Its customers include Bennett Pump, Brunswick Corporation, Dresser Industries, Neway Division of Lear-Siegler, and Shaw-Walker. The firm also serves out-of-town household appliance, automotive, and textile industries.

Donald G. Buehrle, who worked summers in his father's shop while attending high school and college, started with the company on a full-time basis in 1950. Kenneth J. Tyler began on-the-job training as a tool and die apprentice after serving three years in the Navy during World War II. Buehrle Engineering Company, Inc., was incorporated in 1979 with Donald Buehrle as president; Kenneth Tyler, vice-president and secretary/treasurer; and Mrs. Marion Buehrle and Mrs. Dorothy Tyler, directors.

Kenneth J. Tyler, vice-president and secretary/treasurer.

SYTSEMA FUNERAL HOME, INC.

Since 1929 the name Sytsema has been synonymous with funeral home and emergency ambulance service for Muskegon residents. Ambulance service was provided by the firm for more than two decades, ending in 1969. Today the Sytsema family continues to operate two funeral homes.

John Sytsema began his business in 1921, conducting funerals in the family home in Grandville near Grand Rapids. Soon the family moved to McBain near Cadillac, where Sytsema sold furniture in addition to working as an undertaker. His son, Martin, graduated from McBain High School.

The Sytsema family came to Muskegon in 1929 and began its business in a building at Terrace Street and Hartford Avenue. Another funeral home occupies the structure today. Robert Sytsema, grandson of the founder, remembers a story about that first home. His father and grandfather found a large room on the third floor filled with chairs. Later they learned that a club that met there actually was the local chapter of the Ku Klux Klan.

During the Depression the building was repossessed by financiers. Later, John and Martin Sytsema opened a new facility on Apple Avenue at Holt Street. One of the two Sytsema homes is still at that location.

John Sytsema died in 1941, and Martin closed the business when he entered the Army, serving in England during World War II. When Martin returned home, he had a chapel addition built and soon began emergency ambulance service.

By 1969, when ambulance service was discontinued, Sytsema was answering 1,200 calls per year. At that time companies with medically trained and licensed personnel took over the ambulance service that local funeral homes had provided.

Martin Sytsema and Max Walburn merged their businesses in 1976.

The present location of Sytsema Funeral Home, 737 Apple Avenue, as it looked in 1935.

Walburn, who opened his funeral home at 1547 Sherman Boulevard in 1954, retired in 1981. Robert Sytsema, who began working with his father in 1970 and with Walburn in 1976, today manages the Walburn-Sytsema home on Sherman Boulevard. His brother, John, joined the business in 1972 and currently manages the Apple Avenue facility.

Clifford VanderWeg is the senior staff member, with forty years of service to the firm. The three other licensed funeral directors on the Sytsema staff are Robert Vanderlaan, Ross Meyering, and Kenneth Wolffis. All began with the company on a part-time basis while still in high school.

Both Martin and Robert Sytsema have served on the Western Michigan Christian High School Board. Robert was also a director of Hospice of Muskegon and an adviser to Compassionate Friends, a nationwide support group for bereaved parents.

John Sytsema was a member of Muskegon Christian School Board. He also assisted in the formation of HOPING, an organization for parents whose children have died or who need support in caring for terminally ill children.

Martin A. Sytsema

CAMPBELL GRINDER COMPANY, INC.

Campbell Grinder Company was incorporated in 1969 by Hugh H. Campbell to build precision rotary grinding machines. These large machines are custom engineered and designed to meet exacting customer specifications. Only a few machines were built that first year. Campbell now has the help of his two sons, and the company is producing as many as twenty machines a year.

Hugh Campbell and his sons operate the company at 1974 East Sherman Boulevard. They design and supervise the assembling of huge grinding machines built to customer specifications.

Campbell is an old family name in the Muskegon-area business community. Hugh's uncle Donald was one of the founders of Campbell, Wyant, and Cannon Foundry Company. Hugh worked there on a part-time basis as a student. After completing engineering school, he worked for Chevrolet for fifteen years, then returned to Muskegon and worked for the Muskegon Piston Ring Company. In the early 1950s he was chief engineer for the Frauenthal Division of Kaydon, which built grinders to make large bearings.

After that firm was sold in 1961, Campbell held down two jobs. He worked for a local machine shop and at the same time designed components for grinders, which he assembled at his one-man enterprise called Seaway Machinery. In 1969, when the demand for precision grinders outstripped his capacities, he set up shop with four employees in a building at Ninth Street and Keating Avenue in Muskegon Heights.

Norman Campbell, Hugh's oldest son and also a graduate engineer, started with the firm in 1970 and currently is president of Campbell Grinder Company, Inc. Hugh Michael, Hugh's youngest son, began his career with the firm in 1984.

Campbell Grinder built its present plant, at 1974 East Sherman, in 1979. Subsequent growth has doubled the plant's size and has brought about the addition of offices and an adjoining building to house Camtec, a subsidiary that retrofits grinding machines with the latest computerized controls and other technological improvements. Campbell also developed a unique angle slide arrangement for grinding aircraft engine components. It allows working on several surfaces simultaneously with greater accuracy and labor savings.

The firm's work force totaled thirty in 1985. Campbell creates additional Muskegon employment by subcontracting with local businesses to manufacture half of the components used in its machines.

Campbell Grinder pioneered a grinder to form ceramic nose cones for missiles. Many major U.S. manufacturers buy Campbell grinders to shape such products as aerospace and turbine engine components, aircraft/missile radar dome nose cones, space shuttle windshields, submarine seals, and optical telescope mirrors.

The company built a Large Optical Grinder (LOG) on which the University of Arizona, in 1985, was grinding the world's largest one-piece mirror (twenty-two feet in diameter) for a telescope. Weighing fifty-five tons, the LOG was Campbell's largest grinder to date. Another client is the People's Republic of China, which contacted various manufacturers in Europe, Asia, and the United States before contracting with Campbell to build a machine to grind large bearings for its seaport facilities.

An explosion caused extensive damage to the firm's office area on November 23, 1985. No one was injured in the early-morning blast, and employees were back at work the same day.

Hugh H. Campbell, flanked by sons Norman (right) and Michael, with one of the company's precision grinding machines.

A Campbell dual-head vertical grinding machine used to grind jet engine components.

RYKE'S BAKERY

Ryke's Bakery is a Muskegon family business born of the Great Depression. Its founder, John Th. Ryke, received training and experience as a pastry baker and chef in hotels and bakeries in his native country, the Netherlands.

He also worked as a cook on the passenger steamship *Rotterdam.* His last voyage across the Atlantic was in 1915 when he came to America to marry his fiancée, Henrietta, who had emigrated from Holland with her parents a year earlier. The newlyweds settled in Muskegon and built a home on the corner of Larch Avenue and Smith Street.

Ryke's first job in Muskegon was at Campbell, Wyant, and Cannon Foundry. In his twenty-two years at the company he worked his way up to core room foreman. When his hours were cut back at the foundry because of a decline in business in 1932, Ryke was determined to earn more money to support his growing family by doing the work he knew best—baking.

Soon Ryke began baking Dutch butter cookies in the family kitchen. He insisted that only the finest-quality ingredients be used. All the sifting, mixing, stirring, cutting, and other operations were done by hand. Mrs. Ryke and the children, when they were old enough, assisted with the work.

At first he gave samples to neighbors and friends, and the Ryke children took cookies to their schoolteachers and classmates. As word spread of the tasty Dutch treats, the townspeople began to buy the cookies. To keep up with the demand, Ryke soon had to purchase a small oven, a showcase, scales, and a supply of paper bags. Two of the Ryke daughters pulled a coaster wagon to deliver baked goods to customers on Saturday mornings.

Soon orders began to come in by telephone, and Ryke made deliveries with the family car. When she turned fourteen, Marie Ryke, the oldest daughter, obtained a driver's permit and began to make deliveries so that her father could devote more time to baking. At that time Ryke was making four varieties of butter cookies. Each was popular but the thin wafer variety was favored by most customers.

In 1935 Ryke received his first order for a wedding cake. Daughter Marie, then seventeen years old, remembers that the order caused quite a stir and resulted in "something special" for the wedding party. Marie also recalls that word of Ryke's tasty products reached the Sylvan Beach resort area near Whitehall, where several prominent people spent their summers. The most famous customer to visit the bakery was James Roosevelt, son of President Franklin D. Roosevelt.

In 1938 a small garage next to the family home was razed and a bakery was built. That same year Ryke made the decision to quit his foundry job and devote all his efforts to baking. Henrietta, who had experience as a clerk in her father's meat market, and the six Ryke children all helped with the business.

Ryke's Bakery's first employee outside of the family was a retired Dutch baker who worked part time. Later a full-time baker was added, and neighborhood teenagers were hired to work after school and on Saturdays. The product line at this time included special cakes, bread, rolls, and other varieties of pastry.

In 1967 the bakery business was moved into its present location, a remodeled building at Terrace Street and Laketon Avenue that had housed the Sanitary Dairy. Later a Dutch coffee shop serving soup, sandwiches, and baked goods was added to the bakery business in the larger building.

John's son, Henry, and oldest daughter, Marie Borgeson, took over management of the bakery at the time of their father's death in 1967. When Mrs. Borgeson retired in 1981, Henry became the sole owner of the bakery. His wife, Ellen, entered the business in 1982.

According to Ellen Ryke, in early June the bakery produces 300 sheet cakes on peak weekends for parties honoring school graduates. "The demand for wedding cakes is constant throughout the summer," she says, "because halls for wedding receptions are booked throughout the warm weather months, usually a year or more in advance."

In 1938 a small garage next to the family home was razed and the first Ryke's Bakery was built. John Ryke stands in the door of the new establishment.

CWC CASTINGS DIVISION OF TEXTRON, INC.

Fellow foundrymen in the early years sometimes referred to Campbell, Wyant, and Cannon as "the farm boys in Muskegon." The three partners laughed it off and went on about their business of making the best possible castings at the lowest possible price. Eventually they were to build the world's largest independent gray iron foundry and achieve many other distinctions for themselves, their workers, and their community.

Donald J. Campbell, Ira A. Wyant, and George W. Cannon all came from foundry families. Campbell was a third-generation foundryman from Ontario, Canada. Wyant's stepfather was a molder in Muscatine, Iowa, and Cannon's father cast metal in Springfield, Illinois.

As apprentices learning the metal-casting trade, they met in Chicago while working at the Ferguson and Lange Foundry. William Ferguson, the senior partner, had operated Rogers Iron Works in Muskegon, serving sawmills and timber cutters. Ferguson was a tough taskmaster who demanded perfection in his trainees' castings,

Cannon related in a company history, *That First Casting Must Be Good,* which he published in 1964 after retiring. It was authored by Wally E. George, who had worked for Cannon.

Among other things the three young moldmakers learned the intricate task of making cores to cast engine blocks for the infant automobile industry. In their free time they talked business and formed a partnership. Each contributed ten dollars per month to a research fund to be used to plan out the type of foundry business they hoped to start one day.

Campbell came across a classified ad in a trade paper that stated that the Racine Boat Manufacturing Co. brass and iron foundry in Muskegon was available for lease. Owner William Reynolds also would consider a partner. The three foundrymen hurried to Muskegon and looked over the foundry and boatworks that had been built on a one-time sawmill site beside Muskegon Lake. On April 20, 1908, the partners signed a contract agreeing to rent the building for $200 per month, run the foundry, sell engine castings to the boat-building firm, and "draw not more than fifteen dollars per week for their services."

There were struggles at first. Ten other foundries were trying to keep going while sawmills were closing and moving out of town. In addition, the partners' capital was nearly gone. Their first big break came when they produced a test engine block for nearby Continental Motors Corporation. Company executives appreciated the casting's precise dimensions and placed an order for 250 more blocks.

That opened the door to customers in the Michigan-based automobile industry. Business prospered, and employees were hired and trained to make precise castings. On advice of their bankers, the partners incorporated as Campbell, Wyant and Cannon Foundry Co. in 1910.

Overcoming some sales and financial problems, CWC put together enough money to buy one competitor's closed foundry. Enterprise Iron Works, between Sanford Street and the Pere Marquette Railroad Tracks in Muskegon Heights, became Plant 1. The foundry of Pyle Pattern Works across Sanford Street was purchased in 1916 and developed as Plant 2.

CWC built up an impressive list of customers. It included such firms as Reo Motors, International Harvester, Dodge Brothers, and Fordson Tractors. The Muskegon partners also took over management of the faltering National Motors Castings Co. in South Haven, and later merged it into their firm.

World War I production began gradually, reaching a peak near its end in 1918. Plants 1 and 2 were expanded and, with 1,500 men working, reached a top output of 300 tons of castings per day. The firm's production of quality castings won War Department citations. CWC made castings for Army trucks, tanks, tractors, and airplane motors, as well as Navy surface ships and submarine engines.

Campbell, Wyant and Cannon's foundry had become a million-dollar

Organized in 1908, Campbell, Wyant and Cannon Foundry Co. rented this plant from Racine Boat Company.

Donald J. Campbell

Ira A. Wyant

George W. Cannon

business by war's end. Peace brought an increased demand for automobiles. CWC was ready, willing, and able to manufacture cylinder blocks and other components for the dozens of engine and car builders in Muskegon, Detroit, and other Midwest cities.

Prospects of even greater prosperity prompted the founding trio to plan the building of Plant 3. They had purchased a 200-acre tract along Henry Street in Norton Township,

An aerial view of the CWC Castings Division of Textron, Inc.

south of town. Architects were hired to design foundry buildings covering four acres. Worker safety and health facilities were part of the plan, as was the most modern metal-casting equipment available. When it opened in early 1922, the plant was the largest foundry built independently of a related industry.

With its advanced techniques and equipment, Plant 3 became a specialty foundry, producing cylinder blocks, heads, and sleeves; exhaust manifolds; and alloyed steel gears. In addition, CWC gathered expert foundry engineers and production managers to design and produce more and better castings.

Aesthetics and employees' housing needs also were incorporated into plans for the plant. Lawns, shrubs, trees, and flower beds were planted around the buildings. A subsidiary company was set up to landscape and improve the areas south and west of the plant with streets, walks, playgrounds, and a school site; it was named Roosevelt Park.

The three founders continued in their capacities as the company continued to expand. Campbell oversaw the metallurgy and production work; Wyant's specialties were sales and finance; and Cannon's experiments led to several new products. One was the

Centrifuse brake drum in which molten cast iron is fused onto steel rims by centrifugal spinners within electric furnaces to control the alloying process. That innovative process also was used for casting engine cylinder liners and sleeves.

CWC research also came up with a heat-treating process to harden the cam points on cast-iron camshafts. It was a major breakthrough in the metallurgy industry and was kept secret from competitors. Motor manufacturers bought millions of them in 1941. Another development was cast crankshafts that were molded of special steel alloys. Research also developed rocker arms and V-8 engine blocks for Ford cars.

In 1938 the firm staged a thirtieth-anniversary banquet honoring its first employee, Henry Hesby, first foreman, Dennis Sikkenga, and seventeen other veteran workers. Two years later a majority of employees voted in the United Auto Workers as their labor union.

The manufacture of armaments for U.S. and allied forces under the lend-lease program boosted foundry production in 1941. New steel converters and molders were purchased to cast British Army tank track links. In addition, diesel engine blocks for Navy ships and landing craft were made in Plant 1. The Shaw-Box Crane Division foundry in Muskegon Heights, closed in 1930, was renovated and equipped to cast large diesel engine crankshafts for submarines. The foundry later became CWC Plant 4.

Six months before the war ended CWC opened Plant 6 north of Plant 3 to manufacture cylinder sleeves for military engines. Employment at the firm reached an all-time high of 4,840 in 1943. CWC's five Michigan plants turned out 550,000 tons of iron and steel during the war years.

In addition to its gold-star servicemen, CWC lost its founder to the war effort. In 1943 Don Campbell died of a heart attack. The following year directors named Cannon as president of the company and Wyant, vice-president. In 1947 Cannon be-

came board chairman, and Wyant was named president. Wyant retired in 1950, at which time Carl Allen of New York was elected president. Six years later, in 1956, control of the company passed from the two remaining founders when stockholders voted to sell the firm to Textron, Inc., a conglomerate made up of diverse industries.

Richard L. Lindland, a CWC vice-president, became the first president of the CWC Castings Division of Textron in 1956. He was succeeded by John M. Kloap in 1974, with John L. Kelly named president in 1983.

Under new management CWC foundries heated up and cooled down with the nation's economy, peace-keeping wars, and auto industry fluctuations. When car and truck builders floundered in the late 1970s and casting orders slowed, management was forced to lay off workers and close the smaller plants. Plant 1 was the first to go, followed by Plant 4 and the South Haven foundry.

The hardest blow to the company

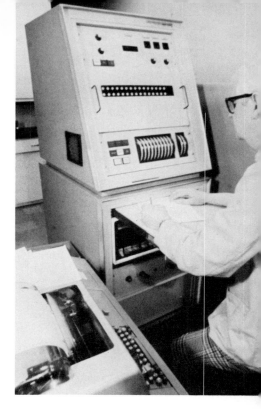

From the firm's beginning in 1908, producing the best castings at the lowest prices has been made possible through constant testing and research.

and Muskegon's economy came in late 1985, when Kelly announced that Plant 3 would be closed within a year and its engine-casting work transferred to a Textron foundry in Columbus, Indiana, near the division's prime customer, Cummins Engines. The plant's 450 foundry workers no longer would cast metal in the big factory. The scheduled 1986 phaseout would leave Plant 5 on Sherman Boulevard and the division offices on South Henry Street still operating.

In his retirement, George Cannon continued his penchant for training young people to run foundries and do a precise job of casting metal. He helped design and install a model foundry in Hackley Manual Training School. When it opened in 1949 on the Muskegon High School campus, he poured the first mold in a casting box. During and after his active years with the company he received honors and citations from colleagues in the industry and universities in Michigan and West Germany, where he had studied and surveyed the metal-casting industry.

CWC developed the cast-steel rocker arm and produced the V-8 engine blocks used by Ford Motor Company in its automobiles of the late 1930s.

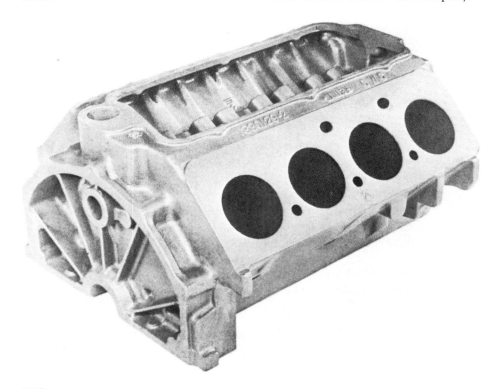

A-1 MACHINE COMPANY, INC.

John H. Matheny and his wife, Dorothy, in front of their A-1 Machine Company shop on Getty Street.

A-1 Machine Company, Inc., is a family-owned and -operated business that does tooling and production work for manufacturers in Muskegon, other parts of Michigan, and elsewhere in the nation. The shop at 181 Getty Street is operated by the Matheny family. Calvin D. Matheny is vice-president in charge of the shop and shares the office work with his mother, Dorothy B. Matheny, secretary/treasurer, who does the bookkeeping. Her husband, John H. Matheny, president of the firm, was incapacitated by severe illness in 1982. Calvin Matheny joined the business in 1968. "My dad got me started, and I learned it all right here in the shop," he says.

In 1985 the number of employees ranged from ten to thirty. Operating such machines as vertical mills and computer numerically controlled lathes, they do tool and die work, production runs, and custom work. The firm uses many kinds of material, including tool steel and other steel alloys, cast iron, aluminum, bronze, brass, and plastics. Both stamped and cast forms of metal are used.

A-1 Machine was founded by Gerald Shugars and Robert Mavis in 1961. The pair set up a machine tool shop in a small building at 821 Fleming Street. John Matheny went to work with the partners a year later after stints at other Muskegon machine shops. Matheny bought Mavis' interest in the business and became the sole owner in 1972.

As business expanded, more space was needed. In 1977 the shop was moved from Fleming Street to its present location on Getty Street. Six months after the move the firm was incorporated.

A-1 Machine works primarily with Muskegon County industries. Its representatives go to local factories to assist with the design of tooling and fixtures to be used in production. Fabrication of prototypes and rebuilding of industrial machines are other services provided by the company.

Teledyne Continental Motors is one of the firm's leading customers. In addition, A-1 Machine built a hydraulic charging cart that was shipped to Jordan to charge the suspension systems of its Army tanks. A-1 also has produced parts for the U.S. Army's HUMVEE vehicle.

When Anaconda Wire & Cable was operating locally, A-1 Machine rebuilt wire spooling machines and developed dies used to wrap paper around wire for that firm. Other Muskegon firms that do business with A-1 Machine Company, Inc., are Sealed Power, Howmet Turbine Components, Dresser Industries' Crane and Hoist Division, Brunswick Corporation, and Textron CWC Castings.

Son Calvin Matheny joined the family business in 1968.

BRUNSWICK®
BOWLING & BILLIARDS CORPORATION

Brunswick Corporation has been producing bowling balls, billiard cues, and accessories in Muskegon since October 1906.

Brunswick Balke Collender Company had been making billiards and bowling equipment and ornate saloon fixtures for sixty years before opening its Muskegon factory. Two prominent Muskegon businessmen, Charles Hackley and Thomas Hume, went to Chicago and convinced Brunswick president Benjamin Bensinger to build his next factory in their town. The factory was opened with ceremony on October 15, 1906. One hundred people were employed to make billiard cues, bowling balls, and accessories.

One industry historian said the Muskegon facility proved to be Brunswick's most important plant in the sixty years that followed. However, many changes had to be made as the company shifted product lines and personnel. The first small factory was expanded to the present sprawling complex on Laketon Avenue at Seaway Drive.

Throughout the years Brunswick hired workers who possessed an inventive bent to develop new products. One such product was the Mineralite hard rubber bowling ball developed by Michael Whelan. Ernest Hedenskoog's years of work to develop an automatic pinspotter led to the design and manufacture of the corporation's first successful device in the 1950s.

Brunswick phonographs, complete with wood cabinets, were first produced in the 1920s. Entertainer Al

Jolson's hit recording of "Sonny Boy" helped get him a seat on the company's board of directors. A line of car tires also was produced.

After Prohibition ended in the 1930s, bar fixtures were manufactured along with refrigerators, freezers, and the first coin-operated Coca-Cola dispensers. World War II production included plywood airplanes, gliders, and landing craft; bombing flares; and tent frames.

When the sport of bowling boomed after the war, factories busily turned out semiautomatic pinsetters, plastic

---

One of the more recent additions to the firm's product line is this electronic scorer.

pins, balls, and wood for lanes; aluminum aircraft parts; school furniture; and folding bleacher seats. Freezer and refrigerator production was also resumed.

The firm's Muskegon facility became part of Brunswick's Technical Products Division in 1967 and manufactured metallic fiber used in Army camouflage nets, jet engines, and carpeting. Products of the 1970s included a new plastic finish for bowling lane surfaces and electronic scorers.

Brunswick moved its Bowling & Billiards division offices from corporate headquarters in Skokie, Illinois, to Muskegon in 1983, and later made the division a wholly owned subsidiary.

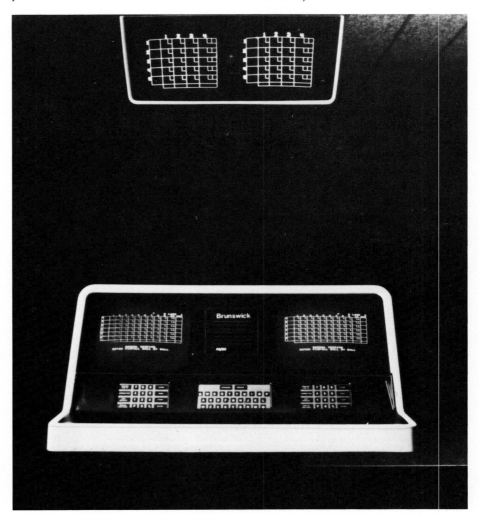

MUSKEGON BUSINESS COLLEGE

The Muskegon Commercial College trained businessmen and businesswomen at Webster Avenue and Jefferson Street from 1908 to 1957.

Founded nearly 100 years ago, Muskegon Business College saw much of its growth take place in the past decade. The school has built teaching and living facilities into an attractive inner-city campus to accommodate nearly 1,500 students.

One reason for the college's success is its outstanding record of job placement for its graduates. MBC is one of only a few independent junior

Robert D. Jewell, president.

colleges in the United States that is entitled to confer degrees. Students may choose from more than thirty courses of study leading to clerical certificates, secretarial diplomas, or associate degrees in business, secretarial, or applied science. Degree programs are offered in such fields as business management, accounting, word processing, marketing, electronic technology, medical records, and drafting.

President Robert E. Jewell and his father, Gail A. Jewell, have been associated with the college since the Great Depression. Gail was the principal commercial teacher when he purchased the school from Arthur Howell in 1932.

The college was founded in 1888 by W.N. Ferris, a former senator who owned a business school in Big Rapids. The first classes were held in third-floor rooms of the Gustin Building on Western Avenue. H.W. Rathbun, the institution's first teacher and later its owner, sold the school to Edward Bisson who moved it to a building at Western and Third Street. Bisson constructed his own facility at Jefferson Street and Webster Avenue and in 1909 started classes on the upper floors. There the school remained for forty-eight years under various owners and names.

In 1965 Robert Jewell moved from teaching to administration, becoming president of the institution. He reorganized the college as a nonprofit corporation and obtained degree-granting authority from the state. MBC added engineering to its curriculum by acquiring Mid-West School of Technology. It later developed a credit transfer and bachelor's degree program in association with Aquinas College in Grand Rapids.

Enrollment grew from 350 in 1975 to 1,450 ten years later. To accommodate the swelling student roster, Muskegon Business College invested several million dollars in developing the modern campus on Apple Avenue at Hartford and Pine streets. The first to be built was the Academic Center, followed by the Library/Administrative building. Housing to accommodate 250 resident students includes three apartment complexes. Also provided are recreation areas and parking for commuter and resident students.

A landscaped campus fronts the Technology Center of Muskegon Business College on Apple Avenue.

HOWMET TURBINE COMPONENTS CORPORATION MISCO

It started as Misco Precision Casting Company—twenty-eight employees making turbojet engine castings in a Whitehall foundry in 1951. Today seven buildings comprise the manufacturing and technological center of Howmet Turbine Components Corporation, Muskegon Operations.

The firm produces castings for aircraft jet engines and other gas-powered turbines, in addition to titanium ingots and superalloys. Based in Greenwich, Connecticut, Howmet is recognized as a world leader in the production of investment castings for the aerospace industry. In 1976 the company became a subsidiary of Pechiney Ugine Kuhlman, a French multinational firm with primary interests in metals and nuclear fuels. The Whitehall center's newest building, the Manufacturing Engineering Division, is regarded as the top research and development center for investment cast jet engine components in

This was the firm's first plant in Muskegon County in 1950.

the world.

Michigan Steel Castings Company (Misco) was moved from Detroit to Whitehall the year after the Korean War began. The firm's first jobs were molding castings for jet engines in Curtiss-Wright and Pratt & Whitney military and civilian aircraft. When Boeing 707 jets went into commercial service, Misco had a head start in manufacturing the engine castings because of prior experience producing parts for B-52 bomber and KC-135 jet engines.

There were many improvements in manufacturing and technology during Howmet's first three decades. The 1960s saw the machining of investment castings and diffusion coating to retard the abrasion of turbine components. The next decade saw the addition of ceramic pouring crucibles to the product line, the reclamation of Mono-Shell castings material, and the installation of hot isostatic pressing equipment to strengthen castings to resist wear. Titanium metal casting was also expanded. Howmet put robots to work

for the first time in 1980, dipping Mono-Shell molds. Laser beams were used to weld and drill components. In 1983 Howmet created a turbine refurbishment operations to repair engine components and extend their life.

Howmet operated for twenty years in the cities of Muskegon and Muskegon Heights. Castings were made in the old Amazon Building on Western Avenue beginning in 1956. Three structures at Seventh Street and Park Avenue in Muskegon Heights were used for casting, finishing, and shipping. These operations were moved to the firm's Hampton, Virginia, plant by 1975. Executive offices were located in Muskegon's Terrace Plaza Building until 1982, when the move to Greenwich was completed.

The Muskegon Operations are made up of seven buildings in two groupings—Misco Drive between Mears Avenue and White Lake, and the Howmet Industrial Park a few blocks east at Benston and Warner roads. Misco Drive plants were con-

Additions to the plant were under way when this photo was taken in 1952.

structed around the original foundry, which was expanded several times. Plant 1 houses directional solidification (component life extending) facilities, office services, and the personnel department. Next door is the data center, a renovated warehouse. Across Misco Drive, Plant 3 is devoted to the production of aircraft engine parts and also houses offices.

Industrial park facilities include Plant 4, housing Whitehall Machining, Thermatech, and Titanium Ingot divisions; Plant 5, occupied by International Operations, and the Ceramic Products and Ti-Cast divisions; Plant 8, the Manufacturing Development and Engineering Division; and the Technical Services Center.

Howmet castings are built into jet and turbine engines that propel space and defense vehicles, aircraft, and missiles. Directionally solidified blades and integrally cast turbine nozzles help control the Space Shuttle *Columbia's* three main engines. HTCC components also go into Navy F-18 Hornet carrier-based fighter jets and the gas turbines that power the Army's newest tank, the M-1 Abrams.

Commercial applications include gas turbines that energize offshore oil-drilling platforms and electric power generating stations, and the Boeing 747's four jet engines.

Theodore "Ted" Operhall, a former Misco executive, was named president of Howmet's Gas Turbine Components Group headquartered in Whitehall in 1973. He was elevated to chairman of the board and chief executive officer in 1978 when Charles Yaker was named president. Yaker retired in 1985, at which time directors named Joseph L. Mallardi president and chief executive officer.

The management of Howmet Turbine Components Corporation has encouraged employee participation in identifying and solving work problems through a team program called Quality Circles. The firm also maintains a ten-acre park for employees and their families. Facilities include a picnic area, tennis courts, softball diamond, and fitness trail. In addition, the corporation financed the restoration of an old theater on Mears Avenue near the Whitehall business district. Named Howmet Theater, it provides facilities for area drama and musical groups.

The home of the Whitehall Casting Division of Howmet Turbine Components Corporation.

CITY OF MUSKEGON

Muskegon's municipal history is the tale of a town whose citizens put boards, beams, and bricks together and joined the villages and settlements along the south side of Muskegon Lake to form the city.

Most of the cosmopolitan community's civic and political development took place after the Civil War. Early settlers built homes near the waterways before Michigan became a state in 1837. The cluster of homes and shops along the southeast elbow of the lake was organized as a village in 1861. Lyman G. Mason, the village's first president, later served as a city alderman and mayor.

In 1869 villagers voted to incorporate as a city. Chauncey David was Muskegon's first mayor. He and the common council of three ward aldermen first convened April 9, 1870, and set about planning improvements for the new city.

Both Western Avenue and Water Street were planked with pine lumber, and a hospital was built to care for smallpox patients. The council also adopted an ordinance that prohibited dumping trash in or otherwise polluting Beidler Creek, the public water supply. Following a disastrous fire in 1874, city fathers sought a larger water supply and piping to carry it throughout the town. A pumping station to draw water from Lake Michigan was built on the bluff and put into operation in 1891.

Lakeside Village and the unincorporated Bluffton and Port Sherman areas near the channel were annexed to the city in 1889. Ethnic and neighborhood settlements taken in later included Rotterdam; Amsterdam, also known as Dutchtown; Pinchtown and Brewery Hill between the city and Lakeside; and Kilgrubbin, later known as Jackson Hill.

The first city hall, built in 1882 at Jefferson and Clay Avenue also housed central police and fire stations. Fire-

The lights of the city brighten the downtown area.

men were hired to man the horse-drawn steam pumper engine, and policemen assisting the city marshal were paid two dollars per day.

By the turn of the century, electric trolleys had replaced the horse-drawn streetcars. A later proposal to replace trolleys with motor buses created so much controversy that the council set a special election in 1921. Streetcars won four to one, but within eight years buses had replaced the last trolleys. Public transportation continued sporadically until the 1970s, when the present county-sponsored bus system was begun.

In 1918 the city went bankrupt, unable to meet its payroll or pay its bills and defaulting on bond payments. Citizens reacted with an overwhelming vote the next year to replace the mayor-council with a city commission-manager form of government. Muskegon was among the first U.S. cities to adopt the new concept of local government. Mayor Paul R. Beardsley and fellow commissioners hired I.R. Ellison away from nearby Grand Haven as Muskegon's first professional manager, and set out to correct the financial problems.

Muskegon's worst flood occurred on February 22, 1922. Rain poured down for two days on top of snow and ice, washing out streets, bridges,

and sewer lines. For several days firemen and city crews pumped out basements and repaired washouts.

City voters in 1931 approved a million-dollar bond issue to finance public works projects and lessen the welfare rolls lengthened by the Depression. In 1946 the city established a planning department to coordinate future growth and the renewal of decaying residential and business areas.

Working with the county and fed-

Small picturesque parks can be found in city neighborhoods.

The Robert Lighton Memorial Park.

eral government agencies, the private sector, and financial interests, the city developed the Marquette and Froebel neighborhood housing projects, the Muskegon Mall and its related improvements, and the rebuilding of Terrace Street. The present city hall, a three-floor structure built in 1970, houses city administrative offices and the police department. The central fire station was opened in 1929 and is across Walton Street from city hall.

Grass-roots government has long been a popular concept in Muskegon. Many citizens have served the city in elected and appointed offices and on the twenty-six boards that give the private citizen a voice in municipal operations. They include planning, civil service, historic district, and housing commissions; parks and recreation, and tax assessment review, building code, and zoning appeals boards; and the Tax Increment Finance Authority.

Currently seven city commissioners are elected on a nonpartisan, combination ward and at-large basis for staggered four-year terms. From its members, the commission elects a mayor and vice-mayor and sets policy through five committees: finance, public facilities, community relations, community and industrial development, and legislative. City commissioners also appoint the city manager, auditor, and attorney. The city manager is responsible for all operating departments, which are grouped into the areas of finance, public works, police, fire, leisure, planning and community development, and administration.

In 1986 Muskegon's government was headed by Mary C. Jones, the city's second female mayor, with Daniel C. Oglesby as vice-mayor. The commissioners were William B. Bailey, Thomas C. Higgins, Stephen C. Holdeman, former mayor Elmer J. Wolcott, and John H. Williams. Robert Hagemann III is city manager.

Muskegon City Hall.

MUSKEGON AREA INTERMEDIATE SCHOOL DISTRICT

Access to an education is a citizen's basic right. This tenet has guided the development of Muskegon County's public schools.

From a one-room facility built for village children in 1849, today's diversified school system, which serves approximately 32,000 students in twelve local districts, has evolved. Another 3,000 pupils are enrolled in parochial and private schools.

Public schools offer everyone from preschool youngsters to senior citizens a variety of programs. Education is a multimillion-dollar-per-year business employing 100 administrators and nearly 1,600 teachers, with taxpayers' investment in buildings and property amounting to several million dollars.

The Muskegon Area Intermediate School District (MAISD) coordinates programs, provides administrative support, and links the local districts with the State Department of Education. The twelve local school districts in the county are Fruitport, Holton, Mona Shores, Montague, Muskegon,

Twelve local school districts make up the Muskegon Area Intermediate School District.

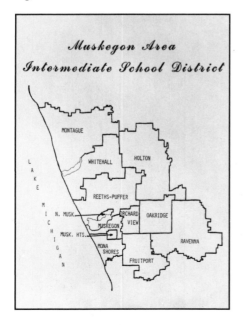

Fourteen youngsters attended Maple Ridge Elementary School in 1914. From left (front row) are Beatrice Brogen, Louella Beys, Carl Sherman, Albert Olsen, Albert Ninehuis, and Katie Cowles. Middle row: Joe Cowles, Dorothy Eckman, and Marie Halley. Back row: Lowell Baars, Clair Black, Violet Olsen Bachmann, Mary Cowles, and Rosa Dorr.

Muskegon Heights, North Muskegon, Oakridge, Orchard View, Ravenna, Reeths-Puffer, and Whitehall. All provide kindergarten through twelfth-grade programs.

Public education in Muskegon can be traced back to 1849 when the first one-room school was erected on the corner of Clay Avenue and Terrace Street. Larger institutions were built as the village grew into a thriving lumbering community. A portion of the wealth accumulated by the lumber barons, especially Charles Hackley, went to support education and the arts in the 1880s and 1890s. Architectural evidence of this era includes Hackley School, Hackley Library, and the Muskegon Museum of Art along Webster Avenue. The Hackley Manual Training School, built on the campus of Muskegon High School, is another example.

Education developed on a different scale and at a slower pace in rural areas. At the turn of the century, close to 100 school districts were in operation. Most children of elementary school age attended the familiar one-room red brick schoolhouse or one

built of wood and painted white.

One of these country schools has been preserved for use by teachers and pupils as a living history lesson. Maple Ridge School on Buys Road in Laketon Township was built in 1877. One hundred years later it was given to MAISD, which administers its operation through a full-time teacher/coordinator. Elementary classes visit the school to relive the days of the three Rs and the hickory stick.

Educators credit Muskegon with historic achievement in three fields—pioneering kindergarten classes fifty years before most schools in the nation and developing vocational education and special education programs before most other Michigan school districts. Special programs for mentally impaired and physically

The intermediate district provides twelve local schools with computer services such as financial accounting, payrolls, grade reporting, and student scheduling. Here operations supervisor Douglas Swanson works at a video terminal.

handicapped students were begun in 1958 and expanded to the preschool and young adult levels in 1971.

In addition, occupational training is offered in local high schools and through a cooperative effort known as the Muskegon Area Vocational Consortium. Students from nine participating high schools receive instruction and hands-on experience in fifteen job fields including courses in auto and small engine repair, computer operation, welding, graphic arts, and electronics.

An academic consortium has been organized to offer courses in Latin, advanced mathematics, and theater. Classes for talented and gifted students are held at the community college. MAISD also coordinates programs in the performing, visual, and literary arts. Adult and community education programs provide basic education and high school equivalency diplomas, skill training, enrichment,

and recreation.

Muskegon area students have consistently done well academically. College test scores show area high school students rank well above the state average academically, while Michigan students rank higher than the national average. In 1984 half of the county's public high school graduates were enrolled in college.

The office of county school commissioner was established in 1867. Between 1905 and 1962 the county board of supervisors approved the annual budget and appointed the superintendent. In 1947 the structure was changed to a county board of education whose members were elected by

local school boards. The board of education would, in turn, elect a superintendent. In 1962 Michigan reorganized all area and county units as intermediate districts.

Local schools have evolved from over 100 schools at the turn of the century to the twelve comprehensive school districts making up the Muskegon Area Intermediate School District. Through local control and cooperation, the Muskegon area schools are among the best in the state and the nation.

A courtyard graces part of the campus of Muskegon Senior High School.

PRO-GAS SALES AND SERVICE COMPANY

M.L. McHenry, a fifty-year veteran in the Michigan oil and gas refining industry, together with his son and two grandsons operate Pro-Gas Sales and Service Company at 1535 South Walker Road. The firm is a leading western Michigan propane gas dealer and supplier, serving industrial, commercial, and residential customers.

McHenry, better known as "Mac," at seventy-nine years of age is an active president and board chairman. His son, William B. "Bill," is general manager of the three-outlet business. A grandson, Ryan, manages the Muskegon operation, while another grandson, Phillip, has charge of fleet service and testing.

In 1937 Mac McHenry moved his family to Muskegon from Enid, Oklahoma, where he was a chief electrician for an oil refinery. His new assignment was to wire controls in a processing unit at the Old Dutch refinery that was processing petroleum from Muskegon-area wells. He stayed three years as plant electrician, then moved to Grand Rapids to run a natural gas stripping plant near Standale. There, liquid gas was sold to customers and natural gas pumped through a pipeline to Muskegon industries.

Near the start of World War II McHenry was asked to dismantle the plant (owned by Pent-Hex Company, a division of West Michigan Consumers Corporation), move it north to Reed City, Michigan, and supervise the construction of a larger facility. Within a year McHenry had the plant pumping liquid and gaseous fuel. It was the first natural gas plant in Michigan to produce propane gas for commercial and home use.

The plant's natural gas output was piped to Muskegon's booming war production factories, which could not get enough fuel from the local gas utility. In the 1930s West Michigan Consumers Corporation had set up a Muskegon plant to recover natural gas from the local oil field. McHenry then moved back to Muskegon to operate the plant, which received natural gas from Reed City. The firm and plant on North Getty near Holton Road were sold to Michigan Consolidated Gas Company in 1946.

With natural gas in short supply because of the postwar business boom, the local gas utility company began to install propane gas systems as backup fuel sources for its industrial customers. McHenry saw the business potential and incorporated Pro-Gas Sales and Service Company on August 7, 1947, with three partners: Harry W. Jones, owner of Jones Electric; Edward C. McLean; and Glen H. Massey.

The firm's first customer was Muskegon Motor Specialties, which used the gas to harden engine camshafts.

Initially McHenry supervised a contracting division of Jones Electric Company, which installed standby propane units for businesses throughout western Michigan, Illinois, and Wisconsin. His son, Bill, along with a couple of hired men, dug ditches, threaded pipe, and installed burner units at residential and commercial installations in areas beyond the reach of the gas company lines.

McHenry's wife, Faye, did the office work in the basement of the family home at Sanford Street and Southern Avenue.

By 1950 the business had returned enough profit to support the family, and the McHenrys purchased the other three owners' interests. The business was then moved across Walker Road to a new building. Later a second floor was added, the exterior remodeled, storage facilities increased, and the delivery fleet enlarged.

To acquire new customers the McHenrys moved into the aerosol packaging industry in 1956. Environmental scientists had warned that extensive use of fluorocarbon sprays could damage the ozone layer of the atmosphere and advised that hydrocarbons should be used in pressurized spray cans. Pro-Gas continues to supply the preferred propellant to manufacturers of hair spray, shaving cream, paint, lubricants, and automotive products.

In 1959 Pro-Gas established a sales and distribution outlet in West Grand Rapids and purchased the Home Utility Co. of Hart, Michigan,

The chief executive officer and general manager of Pro-Gas Sales and Service Company, a McHenry family enterprise, is William B. McHenry (left); M.L. McHenry serves as board chairman.

in 1964. By 1986 twenty-eight persons were employed at the three locations.

In addition, the firm provides engineering and construction services for industrial furnace and oven applications, such as annealing furnaces used to heat treat metal castings. Pro-Gas also offers consulting services to the liquefied petroleum gas industry. Technical background information is available in liability cases stemming from fires, explosions, and similar accidents. The firm provides investigation, research, and expert witness testimony in legal cases.

Ryan K. McHenry, vice-president/operations.

Erdene M. McHenry (left), corporate secretary, and Faye M. McHenry, corporate treasurer.

mental affairs. This resulted in his appointment by the governor to represent the industry on the State Fire Safety Board. Being reappointed for two additional terms, it is a post he still holds. The board is responsible for promulgation of the state fire code as it affects schools, hospitals, nursing homes, and the transporting of chemicals and other hazardous materials. It also serves as an appeal body for those charged with code violations.

Closer to home, William McHenry has served for thirteen years as a trustee on the Mona Shores School Board and two terms as president. He also has been president of the Muskegon County School Board Officers' Association.

Craig W. McHenry, another son of William B., is a mechanical engineer heading up a division of the Applied Physics Laboratory of Johns Hopkins University in Laurel, Maryland.

All three generations of the McHenry family have served the Michigan Liquefied Petroleum Gas Association. Mac was the second man to head the fledgling group in the 1940s; Ryan is currently a director; and William has been an active member for thiry years, serving as president from 1976 to 1978.

William's work in the MLPGA was primarily concerned with govern-

Phillip R. McHenry, vice-president/fleet management.

HOUSE OF TRAVEL, LTD.

Linda Andrews keeps eight pennies in a small picture frame on her desk. The coins remind her of why she went into business with her sister, Patricia A. Bard. The pair opened House of Travel, Ltd., on December 1, 1976, at 935 West Broadway Avenue in Roosevelt Park. Today their firm is considered Muskegon's largest travel agency.

Andrews relates that she had been working long hours at the Muskegon branch of a Grand Rapids travel agency, supporting herself and two small children. After a particularly hectic day, she called the agency owner and asked for a raise. He gave her a figure.

"I got out my little calculator and found it amounted to eight cents an hour!" she recalls. Still fuming, Andrews drove to Bard's home and informed her they were going into the travel business themselves.

Both sisters had previous experience in the travel field. Bard, after teaching school in Hawaii, worked for Capital (later United) Airlines and later joined a local travel firm.

Patricia A. Bard (left) and Linda L. Andrews are two sisters who pooled their resources and expertise to open their own travel agency, House of Travel, Ltd.

An employee sits in front of a floor-to-ceiling map of the world, a fitting background for the agency's Leisure Travel Department.

Andrews worked for one year as a stewardess for United Airlines and then was employed by a Chicago-based travel agency before returning to Muskegon.

The pair found an office and redecorated it with the help of family and friends. Within a month of the opening they hired their first assistant, Christie Bloomer, who is still on the staff. Five more women were hired during the agency's first year in business.

The sisters began the agency with the thought of training all their employees to provide the traveling public with the most professional service possible. That policy continues in the form of weekly staff meetings, training sessions, and seminars in the services offered by airlines, cruise lines, hotels, tour operators, and car rental firms. The agents also get first-hand experience with tours and cruises. In addition, House of Travel offers a lending library of books on tour destinations throughout the world. Travel booking has been computerized since 1979.

The agency moved to 2812 Glade Street, Muskegon Heights, in 1979. The sisters designed the new office building and in 1985 expanded the accounting department and executive offices. Today House of Travel, Ltd., is staffed by twenty-one people.

Both Andrews and Bard serve on the Muskegon Area Chamber of Commerce's transportation committee as well as the Convention and Visitors Bureau advisory board. Pat Bard received the chamber's Entrepreneur of the Year Award in 1983. Andrews is a member of the board of directors of Junior Achievement. Bard is a trustee of Muskegon Community College and a member of the Muskegon County Airport advisory board.

J&M MACHINE PRODUCTS, INC.

J&M Machine Products, Inc., came into existence because of Joseph F. Rahrig's strong sense of business independence. He discovered from experience that he wasn't cut out to be in business with a partner.

Rahrig was a partner in the Engle Machine Company before deciding he would do better on his own. The partnership was dissolved in 1955. That year he and his wife, Mary, started machining metal in a two-stall garage in which the previous occupant had made potato chips. The small building was on the site of the firm's present shop at 1821 Manor Drive.

The couple's initials formed the name of their new business. Mary Rahrig helped by running machines in the shop as well as doing all the record keeping and office work. From that humble beginning, J&M Machine Products has grown into one of Muskegon's leading machine shops. Today the firm offers purchased finished precision-machined parts

to customers throughout western Michigan.

The couple's son, Joseph J. Rahrig, joined the family business in 1966. He became president of the company in 1983 following the death of his father. A 1966 graduate of Central Michigan University, Joseph Jr. began to develop a quality-control program and initiated a marketing thrust aimed at manufacturers in Muskegon County and throughout western Michigan.

J&M Machine Products was a four-man operation until 1964, when the firm received a long-term production run contract. Tooling up for the job cost more than anticipated, and J&M came within one month of bankruptcy before the manufacturing process and marketing became efficient enough to make it profitable.

Joseph F. Rahrig (left) and his son, Joseph J., go over a precision machining operation done at their J&M Machine Products plant in 1976.

As Joseph J. Rahrig's marketing campaign bore fruit, the firm's sales and payroll expanded proportionately. J&M employed twenty-five persons in 1975 when Rahrig moved the firm into a program of state-of-the-art, high-technology machine work.

A Mazatrol M-1 horizontal machining center is computer equipped to provide high-speed, high-accuracy performance. Two vertical machining centers are equipped with computer numerical control, and four lathes have Mazatrol T-1 controls.

In 1985 J&M Machine Products, Inc., employed fifty-five persons. One of the first employees, Robert Lindstrom, is currently vice-president of the company. He began work at J&M following high school graduation in 1957.

Joseph J. Rahrig believes in giving back to the community that is home to his business. He currently serves as a director of Muskegon Catholic Central Foundation, which assists parochial elementary schools and Muskegon Catholic Central High School with operating, scholarship, and capital expenses.

State-of-the-art, high-technology machine work is performed at the firm's 1821 Manor Drive facility.

ECONOMIC DEVELOPMENT CORPORATION OF THE CITY OF MUSKEGON

The Economic Development Corporation of the City of Muskegon was organized in January 1975 to coordinate the intricate finances needed to complete construction of the Muskegon Mall. A decade later the EDC remains in business, collecting rent for publicly funded commercial buildings. That money then goes to meet the mall's financial obligations such as construction loans.

Preliminary work on the multi-million-dollar project already was under way when the EDC was formed to consolidate financing obtained from city, county, and federal agencies; banks; and local businessmen. State legislation enacted a few months earlier permitted cities to form nonprofit corporations for urban redevelopment purposes.

Alan J. Workman, who had headed the Greater Muskegon Civic League, was named president when the EDC was formed. Other EDC officials named at the time include city commissioner Bernard G. Heethuis, vice-president, and Fred C. Culver, secretary/treasurer. In addition, all civic league assets were turned over to the EDC.

The movement that eventually resulted in construction of the mall got its start in 1963.

But the foundation upon which the EDC rests was laid even earlier—in 1960—when several Muskegon manufacturers, with professional research by David Walborn, began exploring why United Way couldn't reach its goals, why support for the West Shore Symphony was dwindling, and why unemployment was so high, particularly among blacks.

Study revealed that Muskegon's unemployment was Michigan's highest; that Muskegon was the state's from which young people were migrating; that its central business district was decaying.

Those findings led to formation of the Muskegon Area Economic Planning and Development Association, a private organization backed by all local banks and industries plus some commercial and professional firms. MAEPDA undertook deeper analysis of the community's social, cultural, and economic dimensions.

It disclosed an impending economic crisis plus serious human and natural resources problems. These findings were publicized in a ten-article *Muskegon Chronicle* series, *Anatomy of An Economy* and a separate book, *Anatomy of A Community*.

Meanwhile, the chamber of commerce was reorganized as the Muskegon Area Development Council. MADC acted not only to begin economic redevelopment, but also to encourage warring local governments to cooperate in seeking ways to end serious county-wide water pollution. MADC also operated a human development division, devoted to improving race relations and halting the decay of old, innercity neighborhoods.

Through MADC, in fact, Muskegon confronted its human and environmental problems well before the heyday of President Lyndon B. Johnson's Great Society program unleashed "massive federal spending." MADC operated on the premise that Muskegon could deal with Muskegon problems far more satisfactorily than far-away bureaucrats and lawmakers. Certainly, during the "long hot summers" of the late 1960s, Muskegon residents suffered neither racial strife nor civil disorder.

Primarily through MADC's research, local leadership, and intergovernmental diplomacy, Muskegon County also led Michigan and the nation in showing not simply how to "treat" water pollutants, but how to clean lakes and streams. The Muskegon County Wastewater system—in essence a farm using polluntants as fertilizers—is the result.

During this same community reawakening, a group of downtown businessmen—many of them the same leaders who formed MADC—issued a call for the general improvement of the blighted central business district.

Within three years a consensus developed that part of Western Avenue should be redeveloped and revitalized

Western Avenue, looking east from Second Street, was enclosed in the early 1970s as a major part of Muskegon Mall.

as a shopping district.

Voters endorsed the city's urban-renewal plan. Federal approval of and funding for the initial project led to the acquisition of property by the condemnation and demolition of buildings. When federal funding was cut back, the city turned to local financial institutions for support. The new Muskegon Corporation was formed and obtained seed money from four local banks to start work on a revised design for the shopping center. Three banks later pledged funds, and two drives were staged to obtain additional financing.

In 1974 the Greater Muskegon Business League, organized to replace the New Muskegon Corporation, signed leases with Sears and Steketees as anchor stores for the mall. A utility tunnel traversing the four blocks of Western Avenue was finished, and a ground-breaking ceremony in late 1974 marked the start of construction.

It was at this point that the EDC came into being and obtained a temporary loan from the city to begin construction of store buildings and the mall itself. Later loans from the city, county, and four banks, in addition to federal Department of Housing and Urban Development grants under Community Development Block and Urgent Need programs, completed the financing for the mall.

Public financing of the project amounted to forty million dollars. That figure does not include the privately owned buildings that were renovated to become part of the business center. Building demolition to make way for new structures was topped off in 1975 when the six-floor Occidental Hotel was dynamited to rubble in seconds by a professional wrecking crew.

Hundreds of shoppers, citizens, business leaders, and government officials participated in the mall's dedication ceremonies on March 26,

1976, which also marked the opening of the anchor and five satellite stores. Within three months fifteen additional shops were opened.

Today Muskegon Mall covers twenty-nine acres in the area bounded by Morris and Clay avenues and Terrace and Third street. The four blocks of Western Avenue are enclosed with glass entrance ways and pyramid skylights, and the entire area has climatized air conditioning. The wide main concourse includes tile flooring, trees, timber pilings, a fountain, and two daises.

Businessmen who headed up the organizations fostering the mall project included Workman, Harold W. Rouse, Max D. Peterson, Heethuis, Culver, Gordon E. Reynolds, and Leo S. Rosen. City officials involved in the project include Mayor Donald E. Johnson, manager Paul F. Frederick, attorneys Harold M. Street and Michael M. Knowlton, and community development director William Gleason. County officials include commission chairman Herman Ivory, vice-chairman John R. Campbell, and administrator Ralph W. Precious.

The mall is unique for several reasons. One is that it is built in the

main retail business section instead of outside of town. Five new structures were melded with four existing buildings into a modern retailing center. In addition, the financing arrangement involved both public and private-sector funds. The mall is also surrounded by some 2,400 free parking spaces.

New buildings have sprung up around the perimeter of the project. They include the Muskegon Federal Savings & Loan building and Terrace Plaza office building, which houses the world headquarters of the Sealed Power Corporation. Other commercial buildings in the downtown area have been renovated and remodeled.

The Muskegon Mall has become a showplace and the center of community activity in its ten years of operation. Annual shows of new cars, boats, recreation vehicles, antiques, arts and crafts, and school achievements are held in the main concourse. High school bands, choruses, and local and visiting musical groups perform on the two daises.

Once Western Avenue looking west, this is the main concourse of Muskegon Mall.

WEST MICHIGAN STEEL FOUNDRY, INC.

West Michigan Steel Foundry, Inc., is a new company with a name, location, and history dating to 1918. That was the year that a business by the same name began casting steel in the foundry on the west end of Western Avenue. In 1963 it became the Muskegon Cast Metals Division of Westran Corporation.

Faced with a possible phase-out by its existing or prospective owner, a group of managers purchased the foundry operation from Westran, effective June 1, 1985. Thirty-five of the division's employees invested as stockholders, and the historic name West Michigan Steel Foundry was revived.

Members of the management team who incorporated the new firm are Gary D. Counselor, board chairman and chief executive officer; David H. Walborn, president and chief financial officer; Reginald Pennington, executive vice-president/engineering; and J. Scott McLaughlin, executive vice-president/manufacturing. Charles J. Perry later became corporate treasurer.

West Michigan Steel Foundry uses nearly every core and mold medium available to the foundry industry today, including green sand, hot shell, colshel, and airset. It uses both arc and induction furnaces to melt carbon, low-alloy, and high-alloy steels, including stainless and manganese. It has the capability to produce castings ranging in weight from ounces to over 2,000 pounds.

Customers have depended over the years on the company's quality-assurance facilities. They include in-house computerized spectrographic equipment, heat treating, and industrial X-ray equipment. Tensile and Charpy impact testing, along with Rockwell and Brinell hardness testing, are also a part of procedures when required.

Since the 1985 reorganization, West Michigan Steel Foundry has

added an in-plant machining facility to better serve customers and to be more competitive with domestic and foreign casting sources.

West Michigan Steel Foundry serves a diversified list of original equipment manufacturers in durable goods markets, including construction equipment, agricultural equipment, transportation equipment, mining, material handling, railroad, hydraulics, machinery and equipment,

Typical castings produced by West Michigan Steel Foundry at the time of production. They include castings that are components in rock bits, ordnance equipment, boiler equipment, trailer suspensions, construction equipment, and industrial valves.

The incorporators of West Michigan Steel Foundry, Inc. From left to right are J. Scott McLaughlin, executive vice-president/ manufacturing; Reginald Pennington, executive vice-president/engineering; Gary D. Counselor, chairman and chief executive officer; and David H. Walborn, president and chief financial officer.

oil field, ordnance, and many others. These manufacturers compose a list of who's who in American industry.

As it approaches its seventieth year in Muskegon, this now employee-owned business hopes not only to continue to contribute to the community's employment rolls but to participate fully in many other aspects of the life of the community.

Patrons

The following individuals, companies, and organizations have made a valuable commitment to the quality of this publication. Windsor Publications and the Muskegon Area Chamber of Commerce gratefully acknowledge their participation in *Muskegon County: Harbor of Promise.*

A-1 Machine Company, Inc.*
Action Industrial Supply Co.
American Coil Spring Company*
Apex Welding Gases and Supplies, Inc.*
Bennett Pump Company*
Brunswick®
    Bowling & Billiards Corporation*
Buehrle Engineering Company, Inc.*
Campbell Grinder Company, Inc.*
Cash Way Lumber Co.
City of Muskegon*
Clock Funeral Home*
Cole's Quality Foods, Inc.*
Comerica Bank-Hackley
Computer Process Utility, Inc.
CWC Castings Division of Textron, Inc.*
Raymond W. Dykema
Economic Development Corporation of the City of Muskegon*
Edlen Machinery Co.
Electronic Heat Treating & Mfg. Inc.
Fleet Engineers, Inc.*
Geerpres, Inc.*
Great Lakes Ford, Inc.
Hackley Hospital*
Clyde Hendrick Realtors*

Holcomb Reporting Service, Inc.*
Horizon Group Outlets/West Village
House of Travel, Ltd.*
Howmet Turbine Components Corporation*
Hunter-Hughes, Inc.*
J&M Machine Products, Inc.*
Johnson Technology
Kaydon Corporation*
Lakeshore Machinery & Supply Co.*
Lift Tech International, Inc. Crane and Hoist Operations*
Robert G. Morin
Muskegon Area Intermediate School District*
Muskegon Business College*
Muskegon Glass Company, Inc.*
Muskegon Insurance Agency, Inc.
Muskegon Lumberjacks Hockey Club
Muskegon Surgical Associates, P.C.
Old Kent Bank of Grand Haven
Professional Search Employment Agency
Pro-Gas Sales and Service Company*
Pro-Phone Communications, Inc.*
Reid Tool Supply Company*
Ryke's Bakery*
Sealed Power Corporation*
Seaway Garages Ltd.
The Shaw-Walker Company*
Sytsema Funeral Home, Inc.*
Teledyne Continental Motors General Products*
Viking Tool & Engineering Inc.

West Michigan Steel Foundry, Inc.*
West-Tech Corp./William Seyforth
White Lake Area Chamber of Commerce
WMUS FM/AM Greater Muskegon Broadcasters, Inc.

*Partners in Progress of *Muskegon County: Harbor of Promise.* The histories of these companies and organizations appear in Chapter VII, beginning on page 140.

Bibliography

Bowen, Duane Thomas. *Shipwrecks of the Lakes.* Cleveland: Freshwater Press, 1952.

Boyd, J. Fred. *My 85 Years in Muskegon.* Ravenna, Michigan, 1978.

Boyer, Dwight. *Strange Adventures of the Great Lakes.* New York: Dodd, Mead and Co., 1974.

Chisholm, John, et al. *The Montague Area, 100 Years.* Montague, Michigan: Montague Area Centennial, Inc., 1967.

Conger, Louis H. "Indian and Trader Days in Muskegon." Paper by Muskegon History Club, Hackley Public Library, 1924.

Dunbar, Willis F. *Michigan, A History of the Wolverine State.* Grand Rapids, Michigan: Eerdmans Publishing Co., 1965.

Haight, Louis P. *The Life of Charles Henry Hackley.* 2 vols. Muskegon, 1948.

Hilton, George W. *The Great Lakes Carferries.* Berkeley, California: Howell-North, 1962.

History of Muskegon County, Michigan Chicago, 1882.

Holbrook, Stewart. *Holy Old Mackinaw, A Natural History of the American Lumberjack.* New York: Macmillan, 1938.

Holt, Henry H. "The Centennial History of Muskegon." Typewritten manuscript, Muskegon, 1883.

Ideal Scrapbook. Vols. 1 and 2. Collection of newspaper clippings, 1891-1927. Hackley Public Library.

Keys, Alice Prescott. "The Romance of Muskegon." Series of articles for the *Muskegon Chronicle.* Muskegon, 1937.

Kiel, Violet. "Growth of Water Transportation in Muskegon Harbor." Thesis, Western Michigan University, Kalamazoo, 1962.

Lipka, Wendell L. *Saga of the White River.* Montague, Michigan: J. Dee, Inc., 1979.

————. *Local Climatological Data.* Asheville, North Carolina: National Oceanic and Atmospheric Administration, 1975.

Newnom, Clyde L. *Michigan's Thirty-Seven Acres of Diamonds.* Detroit: The Book of Michigan Co., 1927.

North Muskegon Historical Committee. The Brinen Lumber Company Prints. Muskegon, 1976.

————. *Portrait and Biographical Record of Muskegon and Ottawa Counties, Michigan.* Chicago: Biographical Publishing Co., 1893.

People's Scrapbook. Vols. 1 and 2. Collection of newspaper clippings, 1914-1930. Hackley Public Library.

Read, Frederic. *A Long Look at Muskegon.* Benton Harbor, Michigan: Patterson College Publications, 1976.

Romig, Walter. *Michigan Place Names.* N.p, n.d. Grosse Pointe, Michigan.

Sand in Their Shoes. Muskegon: Bluffton School PTA Historical Committee, 1970.

Sanford, Ambrosia. "Extracts from Letters Written by Mrs. Samual R. Sanford, 1858-1867." Typewritten manuscript, Hackley Public Library.

————. *The White Lake Area Historical District.* Montague, Michigan: White Lake Area Historical Society, 1976.

Wood, Wesley F. "Some Sketches of Early Muskegon Life." Typewritten manuscript, Hackley Public Library.

Yakes, Daniel J. and Hugh A. Hornstein. *The Many Lives of Muskegon.* Muskegon: Muskegon Community College, 1979.

Newspapers and Periodicals

Muskegon Chronicle, Centennial Edition, June 22, 1957

Muskegon Chronicle, Muskegon Centennial Edition, July 10, 1937

Muskegon Chronicle, 125th Anniversary Edition, June 10, 1982

Muskegon Chronicle, Progress Edition, May 19, 1928

Muskegon Daily Chronicle Archives

Muskegon Daily Times Archives

Muskegon News and Reporter Archives

Muskegon Weekly Chronicle Archives

Index